AMERICA'S
PAST AND PROMISE

Primary Sources and Literature

McDougal Littell Inc.
A Houghton Mifflin Company
Evanston, Illinois   Boston Dallas Phoenix

To the Teacher

This resource book provides a variety of materials for extending and enriching the American history course for average and above-average students. The book consists of two types of blackline-master worksheets: primary source readings and readings from literature.

- One primary source reading is provided for each chapter in *America's Past and Promise*. These readings allow students to study the original words of men and women who made history. The questions in each worksheet test the students' ability to think critically about the material presented.

- One reading from American literature is provided for each chapter of the textbook. These selections offer a reading from a classic or modern literary work and are aimed at (1) helping students see connections between historical developments and works of fiction or other types of literature and (2) encouraging students to find pleasure in independent reading.

Answers for the worksheets are provided at the back of this book. Students' answers to questions that call for interpretations, opinions, and judgments will of course vary. For such questions, notes concerning appropriate bases for answers are provided.

Cover design: Corey McPherson Nash

Bleed cover image: Tony Rinaldo (eagle: Tom and Pat Leeson)

Inset photo: The Stock Market Photo Agency/Mug Shots

Printed in the U.S.A.

ISBN: 0-395-70764-1

45678910-B-99 98 97 96

Contents by Activity

Primary Source
and Literature Worksheets

Name _____ Date _____

WORKSHEET 1 The Zuñi Indians of New Mexico   **Primary Source**

Members of the Zuñi tribe of New Mexico were descendants of the
Anasazi people of the Southwest. The Spanish called their apartment-like
dwellings *pueblos,* which is Spanish for "towns." The following description
of the Zuñi Indians was written in 1540 by Melchor Díaz, a Spanish
explorer and government official. It was told to him by his servants, who
were Indians from Mexico and had traded with the Zuñi.

There are seven settlements, each a short
day's journey from the other. . . . They have
houses of stone and mud rudely fashioned.
. . . The houses are of three or four stories;
they say that only a few are of one or two stories. . . . Ten to twelve houses are reached by
one ladder. They keep stores on the ground
floor and live in the upper ones. Beneath the
houses they have some chambers [*kivas*]. . . .
The informants say that when attacked all
the people gather in the houses, from which
they fight, and that when they go to make
war they take shields and jackets made of
dyed buffalo skins, and that they fight with
stone arrows and mallets and with other
arms of wood the nature of which I have
been unable to understand. . . .

There are many tame turkeys. They have
a great deal of maize, beans, and squash.
They keep some shaggy animals like large
hounds . . . in their houses. These they shear
and make of the clip colored wigs they wear,
like the one I sent Your Lordship and also
they make clothes of the same. The men are
of short stature, the women of light color and
good appearance and wear dresses that
reach to their feet. . . . They hang many
turquoises in the ears and also about the
neck and wrists. . . .

They work the soil as is done in New Spain
and carry loads on the head as in Mexico.
Men weave the cloth and spin the cotton.
Salt is procured from a lake two days' journey [away]. . . . The land they say is productive of maize and beans. They have no fruit
trees nor do they know of such. There are
excellent woods; the province has little
water; cotton is not grown locally but is
brought from Totonteac [the Hopi country];
they eat from plates of pottery . . . ; they do
not know what sea fish are nor have they
heard of such. . . . There is great abundance
of wild goats of the color of roan horses. . . .

Three of the seven places are very large,
the other four not. . . . Taking into account
the houses, their size, and how they are con-
nected and the people living in each house,
there must be a great multitude.

*From the memoirs of Melchor Diaz, vol. 2, pp.356–361,
published in* Sixteenth Century North America: The
Land and The People as Seen by the Europeans, *by
Carl Ortwin Sauer. Copyright © 1971 by The University of California Press. Orginally from Colección de
documentos ineditos relativos al descubrimiento, con-
quista, y organización de las antiguas posesiones
españolas de America y Oceania (Madrid, 1864–1884).*

Comprehension

1. Describe the houses used by the Zuñi.
   How did the Zuñi utilize their environment to provide shelter?
2. What sources of food did the Zuñi have?
   What food did they not have?
3. Why would the weapons of the Zuñi be
   considered primitive?

Critical Thinking

4. In what ways was the Zuñi Indians'
   way of life similar to that of the
   Anasazi?
5. This account of the Zuñi was told to
   Melchor Díaz by his Indian servants.
   Do you think it still qualifies as a primary source? Why or why not?

Primary Sources and Literature   1

Name _____   Date _____

WORKSHEET 1 A Náhuatl Song

Literature

Below is a Náhuatl song. Although Náhuatl was the language of the Aztecs, this particular song was created by the people of Teotihuacán, a city that predates the Aztec civilization. Náhuatl was a spoken, not a written, language. The song was finally written down during the time of the early Spanish conquerors but was not translated into English until much later.

> And they called it Teotihuacán
> because it was the place
> where the lords were buried.
> Thus they said:
> "When we die,
> truly we die not,
> because we will live, we will rise,
> we will continue living, we will awaken.
> This will make us happy."
> Thus the dead one was directed,
> when he died:
> "Awaken, already the sky is rosy,
> already sing the flame-coloured guans,
> the fire-coloured swallows,
> already the butterflies fly."
> Thus the old ones said
> that who has died has become a god,
> they said: "He has been made a god there,"
> meaning, "He has died."

From Mexico, *2nd edition, by Michael D. Coe. Copyright © 1962, 1977 by Michael D. Coe. Reprinted by permission of Henry Holt & Company, Inc.*

Comprehension

1. What does the song say will happen to people after they die?
2. This early culture and the Aztec culture which followed it believed in cremation, or burning the dead. What images in the song illustrate that belief?

Connecting History and Literature

Answer one question with a brief essay.

A. What is the value of translating the songs and stories of ancient peoples?
B. What can happen to the message of a song when the song is translated from one language to another?

Name _____ Date _____

WORKSHEET 2 A Muslim's View of Ghana

The West African kingdom of Ghana was at the height of its power from around A.D. 700 to 1000. The information we have about Ghana during that time comes from accounts written by Muslim travelers, merchants, and geographers. The passage below describes Ghana's capital and its role in the gold-salt trade.

The capital of Ghana consisted of two separate towns, situated about six miles apart. The one was reserved for the Muslim population and contained a dozen mosques where many distinguished scholars and learned doctors lived. The other, known as El Ghaba or the Forest, was pagan and the seat of the court. Most of the houses of Ghana were clay huts thatched with straw, but there were also some finer buildings of stone.

El Ghaba took its name from the groves with which it was surrounded. These groves, which were probably little more than thickets of thorn, were jealously guarded against all intruders, for they were the center of the spiritual life of the nation. Here dwelt the priests, who attended the national gods. Here too were the burial places of the kings and the prisons from which none was ever known to return.

Ghana was the largest and the most important market of the Sudan. The reason for its great prosperity was gold, which was in such abundant supply that precautions had to be taken to limit the amount coming on to the open market lest the price should fall too low. This was done by making all nuggets the property of the king, leaving only the gold dust available for the trade.

The people of Ghana obtained their gold from a country called Wangara, a name which for centuries remained wrapped in mystery. According to one traveler, Wangara was an island 300 miles long and 50 broad, surrounded by the waters of the "Nile," a name which early geographers applied to every river of the interior. This "Nile" flowed from east to west and was undoubtedly the Senegal. In Sugust, the hottest month of the year, the river used to rise and flood the island. When the water receded, the local people came to collect the gold left by the floods, and remained there till the water rose again.

On one occasion the foreign merchants tried to discover the source of the gold by treacherously capturing one of the shy people. They secured one prisoner but he died without divulging any information. As the result of this treacherous act the gold trade was interrupted for three years, at the end of which their craving for salt compelled the people to resume it.

From Caravans of the Old Sahara: An Introduction to the History of the Western Sudan, *by E. W. Bovill. Copyright © 1933 by Oxford University Press.*

Comprehension

1. Who lived in El Ghaba? Who lived in Ghana's other capital city?
2. Why did the king make all gold nuggets royal property, while allowing trade only in gold dust?
3. What happened when foreign merchants tried to discover Ghana's source of gold?

Critical Thinking

4. How did the people of Ghana feel about outsiders? Give evidence from the excerpt to support your answer.

Name _____ Date _____

WORSHEET 2 "The Cow-Tail Switch"

WORSHEET should be WORKSHEET

In traditional West African villages, storytelling was an important part of
village life. Stories taught lessons and brought people together. This story
about a father and his sons was passed down through oral tradition.

Near the edge of the Liberian rain forest, on a hill over-looking the Cavally River, was the village of Kundi. Its rice and cassava fields spread in all directions. Cattle grazed in the grassland near the river. Smoke from the fires in the round clay houses seeped through the palm leaf roofs, and from a distance these faint columns of smoke seemed to hover over the village. Men and boys fished in the river with nets, and women pounded grain in wooden mortars before the houses.

In this village, with his wife and many children, lived a hunter by the name of Ogaloussa.

One morning Ogaloussa took his weapons down from the wall of his house and went into the forest to hunt. His wife and his children went to tend their fields, and drove their cattle out to graze. The day passed, and they ate their evening meal of manioc and fish. Darkness came, but Ogaloussa didn't return.

Another day went by, and still Ogaloussa didn't come back. They talked about it and wondered what could have detained him. A week passed, then a month. Sometimes Ogaloussa's sons mentioned that he hadn't come home. The family cared for the crops, and the sons hunted for game, but after a while they no longer talked about Ogaloussa's disappearance.

Then, one day, another son was born to Ogaloussa's wife. His name was Puli. Puli grew older. He began to sit up and crawl. The time came when Puli began to talk, and the first thing he said was, "Where is my father?"

The other sons looked across the rice-fields.

"Yes," one of them said. "Where is Father?"

"He should have returned long ago," another one said.

"Something must have happened. We ought to look for him," a third son said.

"He went into the forest, but where will we find him?" another one asked.

"I saw him go," one of them said. "He went that way, across the river. Let us follow the trail and search for him."

So the sons took their weapons and started out to look for Ogaloussa. When they were deep among the great trees and vines of the forest they lost the trail. They searched in the forest until one of them found the trail again. They followed it until they lost the way once more, and then another son found the trail. It was dark in the forest, and many times they became lost. Each time another son found the way. At last they came to a clearing among the trees, and there on the ground scattered about lay Ogaloussa's bones and his rusted weapons. They knew then that Ogaloussa had been killed in the hunt.

One of the sons stepped forward and said, "I know how to put a dead person's bones together." He gathered all of Ogaloussa's bones and put them together, each in its right place.

Another son said, "I have knowledge too. I know how to cover the skeleton with sinews and flesh." He went to work, and he covered Ogaloussa's bones with sinews and flesh.

A third son said, "I have the power to put blood into a body." He went forward and put blood into Ogaloussa's veins, and then he stepped aside.

Another of the sons said, "I can put breath into a body." He did his work, and when he was through they saw Ogaloussa's chest rise and fall.

"I can give the power of movement to a body," another of them said. He put the power of movement into his father's body, and Ogaloussa sat up and opened his eyes.

"I can give him the power of speech," another son said. He gave the body the power of speech, and then he stepped back.

Ogaloussa looked around him. He stood up.

"Where are my weapons?" he asked.

They picked up his rusted weapons from the grass where they lay and gave them to him. Then they returned the way they had come, through the forest and the ricefields, until they had arrived once more in the village.

Ogaloussa went into his house. His wife prepared a bath for him and he bathed. She prepared food for him and he ate. Four days he remained in the house, and on the fifth day he came out and shaved his head, because this was what people did when they came back from the land of the dead.

Afterwards he killed a cow for a great feast. He took the cow's tail and braided it. He decorated it with beads and cowry shells and bits of shiny metal. It was a beautiful thing. Ogaloussa carried it with him to important affairs: When there was a dance or an important ceremony he always had it with him. The people of the village thought it was the most beautiful cow-tail switch they had ever seen.

Soon there was a celebration in the village because Ogaloussa had returned from the dead. The people dressed in their best clothes, the musicians brought out their instruments, and a big dance began. The drummers beat their drums and the women sang. The people drank much palm wine. Everyone was happy.

Ogaloussa carried his cow-tail switch, and everyone admired it. Some of the men grew bold and came forward to Ogaloussa and asked for the cow-tail switch, but Ogaloussa kept it in his hand. Now and then there was a clamor and much confusion as many people asked for it at once. The women and children begged for it too, but Ogaloussa refused them all.

Finally he stood up to talk. The dancing stopped and people came close to hear what Ogaloussa had to say.

"A long time ago I went into the forest," Ogaloussa said. "While I was hunting I was killed by a leopard. Then my sons came for me. They brought me back from the land of the dead to my village. I will give this cow-tail switch to one of my sons. All of them have done something to bring me back from the dead, but I have only one cow-tail to give. I shall give it to the one who did the most to bring me home."

So an argument started.

"He will give it to me!" one of the sons said. "It was I who did the most, for I found the trail in the forest when it was lost!"

"No, he will give it to me!" another son said. "It was I who put his bones together!"

"It was I who covered his bones with sinews and flesh!" another said. "He will give it to me!"

"It was I who gave him the power of movement!" another son said. "I deserve it most!"

Another son said it was he who should have the switch, because he had put blood in Ogaloussa's veins. Another claimed it because he had put breath in the body. Each of the sons argued his right to possess the wonderful cow-tail switch.

Before long not only the sons but the other people of the village were talking. Some of them argued that the son who had put blood in Ogaloussa's veins should get the switch, others that the one who had given Ogaloussa breath should get it. Some of them believed that all of the sons had done equal things, and that they should share it. They argued back and forth this way until Ogaloussa asked them to be quiet.

"To this son I will give the switch, for I owe most to him," Ogaloussa said.

He came forward and bent low and handed it to Puli, the little boy who had been born while Ogaloussa was in the forest.

The people of the forest remembered then that the child's first words had been, "Where is my father?" They knew that Ogaloussa was right.

For it was a saying among them that a man is not really dead until he is forgotten.

Primary Sources and Literature 5

Critical Thinking

1. What caused the disagreement among the sons of Ogaloussa?
2. Why did Ogaloussa choose his youngest son to receive the cow-tail switch?
3. What is the moral of the story?

Connecting History and Literature

Answer one question with a brief essay.

A. Do you think that this story makes its point effectively? Why or why not?
B. Oral tradition is an important part of many African cultures. What are the advantages and disadvantages of transmitting stories through spoken rather than printed words?

WORKSHEET 3
Magellan's Men Circumnavigate the Globe

Antonio Pigafetta, a young Italian who sailed with Magellan, kept a daily journal of the long and harrowing voyage around the globe. In the following passages Pigafetta recounts the last months of the journey, around the Cape of Good Hope and up the west coast of Africa.

In order to round the Cape of Good Hope we went as far south as forty-two degrees toward the Antarctic Pole. We remained near this Cape for seven weeks with sails furled because of the west and northwest winds on our bow, and in a very great storm. This Cape is . . . the greatest and most perilous cape in the world. . . .

At length, by God's help . . . we passed this Cape at a distance of five leagues [about 15 miles] from it. . . . Then we sailed northwest for two months continually without taking any refreshment or repose. And in that short space of time twenty-one of our men died. . . . And if God had not given us good weather, we should all have died of hunger. At length, constrained by our great need, we went to the islands of Cape Verde.

On Wednesday the ninth of July we arrived at one of these islands, named Santiago, where we immediately sent the boat ashore to obtain provisions, under pretext and color of telling the Portuguese that our foremast had broken under the equinoctial line (although it had been at the Cape of Good Hope) and that, while we were refitting our ships, our captain-general with the other two ships had gone before to Spain. So with our merchandise and these good words we obtained two boatloads of rice. And we charged our men in the boat that, when they were ashore, they should ask what day it

was. They were answered that to the Portuguese it was Thursday, at which they were very much amazed, for to us it was Wednesday, and we knew not how we had fallen into error. For every day I, being always in health, had written down each day, without any intermission. But, as we were told since, there had been no mistake, for we had always made our voyage westward and had returned to the same place of departure as the sun, wherefore the long voyage had brought the gain of twenty-four hours, as is clearly seen. . . .

On Saturday the sixth of September, one thousand five hundred and twenty-two, we entered the Bay of San Lucar, and we were only eighteen men, the most part sick, of the sixty remaining who had left Molucca [the Spice Islands], some of whom died of hunger, others deserted at the island of Timor, and others had been put to death for their crimes.

From the time we departed from that Bay until the present day we had sailed fourteen thousand four hundred and sixty leagues, and completed the circuit of the world from east to west.

From Magellan's Voyage: A Narrative Account of the First Circumnavigation, *by Antonio Pigafetta, in Hakluyt Society Publications, Vol. 52.*

Comprehension

1. How long did it take the ship to round the Cape of Good Hope? Why?
2. Why did the ship's crew not know the correct date?

Critical Thinking

3. Why did the crew of the ship lie to the Portuguese on the island of Santiago?
4. How were the voyages of Columbus and Magellan similar?

WORKSHEET 3 Scott O'Dell, *The Captive* Literature

As the Spaniards began to explore and settle the Caribbean islands and Central and South America, they brought with them Christian missionaries, whose job it was to convert Native Americans to Christianity. Scott O'Dell tells a gripping tale of a young missionary, Julian Escobar, who stands up to the leaders of an expedition when they enslave the island people and force them to mine gold.

By noon Señor Guzmán had collected his band, six in all, as well as the lone Indian who knew where his tribe had hidden in the past and where they were apt to hide now, and Esteban, our translator. At the last minute, though he thoroughly mistrusted me, Guzmán decided that I should also go along.

Don Luis and I were standing at the head of the lagoon, watching members of the crew empty the storehouse. He had decided to move the gold onto the *Santa Margarita* in case the camp was overrun by the Caribs. There was danger in this, because the ruffian crew could take it into their heads to sail off with the treasure while we were ashore. But it seemed to be less than the danger from marauding Caribs. There was another and more important reason as well. The *encomendero* [Spanish agent] who now owned the island might appear and, finding the shed overflowing with gold, rightfully claim it.

Señor Guzmán came up with his band. "We need you," he said, laying a hand on my shoulder. "The savages will believe what you tell them."

"And what will that be?"

"Say that the Caribs have been vanquished, so it's safe to return to their village."

"The Caribs haven't been vanquished," I replied.

Guzmán went on as if I hadn't spoken.

"Say we regret that it was necessary to do away with the cacique [Indian chief]."

"It was not necessary."

"I gave him fair warning."

"Why should you warn him? It's his island and his people. Why should you order him to do anything? You are not a king."

Guzmán's mottled face grew pale.

Don Luis said, "We need the men and the women also. We can't mine without them."

Guzmán swallowed hard but went on, "Say that we forgive them for running away. That we'll share the gold they mine; share and share alike."

"You're a friend. They'll listen to you," Don Luis said.

"I have nothing to tell them."

"Say what Guzmán has told you to tell them."

"I would have trouble speaking the words."

"Then say that we need them." He was growing impatient. "Go. Every moment counts."

I did not move.

"You want the Indians back as much as I do."

I spoke slowly so that there would be no doubt about what I was saying. "The truth is, sir, I don't wish them back. I wish them to stay where they are. Wherever it is, they are far better off than here."

Guzmán held in his hand the musket he had used upon the Caribs. He glanced at Don Luis, as if asking his permission to use it at that moment upon me. He had large white teeth, and his drawn-back lips showed that they were clamped tight together.

The young Indian who had given him information about the tribe's whereabouts was watching. He sat huddled on the ground. Around his neck from ear to ear I saw that he wore a thin red welt.

I listened in silence as Don Luis repeated his request.

"You are a member of this expedition," he

said. "I, Don Luis de Arroyo, Duke of Cantavara y Llorente, am its leader. I have asked you to accompany us on a mission of great importance. You give me evasive answers."

"What makes you think that our Indians will return to their village if only I speak to them? They have been worked close to death. Some, close to a dozen, have died. Many more have sickened from hard work. And now their chieftain has been cruelly slain.

They trust neither you nor Guzmán. They shouldn't trust me."

"But they do trust you."

"That, sir, is the point. They trust me, and I will not betray them."

From The Captive *by Scott O'Dell. Copyright © 1979 by Scott O'Dell, published by Houghton Mifflin Company.*

Critical Thinking

1. What do Guzmán and Don Luis want Julian Escobar to do?
2. What is the attitude of Guzmán and Don Luis toward the Indians?
3. Why does Escobar refuse to go along with the plan?

Connecting History and Literature

Answer one question with a brief essay.

A. What does this excerpt tell you about Spain's goals in the Americas?
B. Why might some Spanish missionaries, such as Escobar in this story, have felt differently about the Indians than other Spaniards did?

WORSHEET 4
Las Casas and the Plight of the Indians

Bartolomé de Las Casas, a Spanish landowner on the island of Hispaniola in the early 1500s, condemned the mistreatment of Indian laborers. The excerpts below are from a book written by Las Casas around 1522.

The Indians were satisfied with little, and with a minimum of cultivation, this fertile land gave them abundant sustenance. In addition being of a delicate constitution, they could not last long in a life which abruptly plunged them into harsh labor. Up to a third died after each six or eight months' work in the mines, which was the time required of a crew to dig enough gold for melting. Who could recount their starvation, affliction and the cruel treatment these unfortunate people received not only in the mines, but wherever they were put to work? . . .

When the Spaniards saw how fast they were killing Indians in the mines, plantations and other endeavors, caring only to squeeze the last effort out of them, it occurred to them to replenish the supply by importing people from other islands and they deceived [the king] with a crafty argument. They notified him . . . that the [islands] close to Cuba and Hispaniola were full of an idle people who had learned nothing and could not be Christianized there. Therefore they asked permission to send two ships to bring them to Hispaniola where they could be converted and would work in the mines, thus being of service to the King.

Excerpts from History of the Indies *by Bartolomé de Las Casas. Translated and edited by André Collard. Copyright © 1971 by André Collard, published by Harper & Row.*

Comprehension

1. What were some of the ways the Indians were mistreated by the Spaniards?
2. What was the attitude of the Spaniards toward the Indians? How can you tell?
3. Did Las Casas believe that the Spaniards wanted to Christianize the Indians? Did he believe the king wanted to Christianize them? Explain.

Critical Thinking

4. Due largely to the efforts of Las Casas, Indian slavery in the Americas was finally abolished in the 1550s. But limited forced labor continued through the early 1600s, and labor in the mines went on even longer. For his efforts, Las Casas was called "a saint" as well as "the devil's advocate and the archenemy of Spain." Explain why.

WORKSHEET 4
Literature

Helen Rand Parish, *Estebanico*

While researching the period of Spanish exploration and colonization of the Western Hemisphere, the historian Helen Rand Parish became interested in the life of Estebanico (also spelled Estevanico). She decided to write a book about Estebanico, whom she called "the first great black man in America." In her novel *Estebanico,* Parish imagined how Estebanico might have told the story of his many adventures. In the following passage, Estebanico and three companions, having escaped from Indians who had enslaved them, begin their long journey through Texas and toward Spanish-held territory.

We were four—three Castilian [Spanish] gentlemen and one African Negro. All four of us grew taller in that flight.

We had all been slaves, and now we were free. So we were equals and we helped each other. Captain Castillo kept up our spirits with his reckless courage; my master Dorantes taught us to remain nobly aloof with the Indians; Cabeza de Vaca meticulously memorized our distances and dates; and I had a special assignment, as I shall detail. We went in the guise of peddlers; each of us bore on his back a bundle of trade goods and simples, only thus could we move freely along the trails. Your Royal Treasurer [Cabeza de Vaca] we chose as our leader, he was the oldest and most prudent, and my master and Castillo were Captains who had served under his command. Wherefore in our councils we deferred to his decisions on our course and strategy, but on the road it was I who led. . . .

I was the one the natives admired and feared, for my imposing height and my beautiful black color. And I was the one who first entered the villages as ambassador, and prepared the Indians for our coming, and searched out the ways we were to travel. For we went inland from the coast, over rugged country and up onto a great High Plain—an endless sea of green and grayish grasses . . . crossed by many hidden trails. And I alone could inquire which trail should be ours. For I knew the Indian speech, while my three Spanish companions still used mostly the sign language; they were not ignorant of the native tongues but there are six languages along that coast, and they had only a smattering of each, whereas I spoke all six fluently. As I have told, I had always a great facility with languages; I spoke Arabic at home in Azamur, and I learned the tongue of the Portuguese when they took our town, and Spanish in the Duke's household in Seville, and now I had been talking with the Indians by word and sign nearly seven years.

So I went ever in advance, bringing and seeking news of the region in constant conversation with the natives. They advised us to travel north and east to the vast prairies where they hunted the thundering herds of woolly humpbacked cows [buffalo]! I could not take those trails, Your Majesty, they led away from New Spain, and I continued northwest instead.

And in the very first tribe we reached on that high grassland, I made the decision that determined the success of our journey. For I overheard the Indians saying that we must surely be shamans (or medicine men) because of my black complexion, which they considered magical, and because of our beards, they being beardless. For this people had a tale or legend—afterward they repeated it to us, though we could never understand it well—about a wandering medicine man named Bad Demon. He was small and dark and bearded, and he would suddenly appear at their doors in dazzling torchlight and show his sinister magical skill as a surgeon: whoever he seized and cut, whether on the arm or the entrails, would be healed in three days, and he could also dislocate and set bones. They feared him greatly, for there were no physicians among them.

Accordingly they received us with eagerness, and a delegation came to us at night—some men suffering great pains in the head; and they besought us, as we were shamans, to cure them.

From Estebanico *by Helen Rand Parish. Copyright ©
1974 by Helen Rand Parish. Used by permission of
Viking Penguin, a division of Penguin Books USA Inc.*

Critical Thinking

1. At first, what disguise did the four men use when they were traveling among the Indians?
2. What special skill did Estebanico have? How did he put it to use?
3. Who did the Indians on the high grassland think the four travelers were? How was this misunderstanding an advantage for the travelers?

Connecting History and Literature

Answer one question with a brief essay.

A. How had Estebanico and the others become slaves of the Indians?
B. Did the Spanish expeditions to North America prove as successful as those in Mexico?

Name _____ Date _____

WORKSHEET 5 The French Claim Land in Quebec   **Primary Source**

Jacques Cartier explored the St. Lawrence River during 1534 and 1535. The following account records events during Cartier's arrival in Gaspé Bay, which lies between the Gulf of St. Lawrence and the St. Lawrence River, in what is now the province of Quebec. The Indians with whom Cartier dealt were probably Huron or Iroquois.

Upon the 25th of the month, we made a cross thirty feet high in the presence of many of the Indians, upon the point of the entrance of Gaspé Bay. We hung a shield with three *fleur de lis* [an emblem of the king of France] on the cross, and in the top was carved in the wood "Glory to the King of France." Then before the Indians we placed it upon the point. As soon as it was up, we kneeled down before them, with our hands toward Heaven, giving thanks to God. We made signs to them, showing them the Heavens, and that our salvation depended only on God. They showed great admiration, looking first one at another, and then upon the cross. And after we returned to our ships, their captain wearing an old bear skin, with three of his sons, and a brother of his with him, came to us in one of their boats. There he made a long speech to us, showing us the cross we had set up, and making a cross with two fingers. Then he showed us all the country around us, as if he were saying that all was his, and that we should not set up any cross without his permission. Then we showed them with signs that the cross was only set up to be a marker showing the entrance to the port, and that we would shortly come again, and bring iron goods and other things, but that we would take two of his children with us, and afterward bring them to the port again. We clothed two of them in shirts, and colored coats, with red caps, and put about everyone's neck a copper chain, which greatly pleased them. Then they gave their old clothes to their fellows that went back again, and we gave to each one of those three that went back, a hatchet, and some knives, which made them very glad. After these were gone, and had told the news to their fellows, six boats came to our ships, with five or six men in every one, to say farewell to those two we had detained to take with us, and brought them some fish, saying many words that we did not understand, and making signs that they would not remove the cross we had set up.

Adapted from Early English and French Voyages, Chiefly from Hakluyt, 1534–1608, *edited by Henry S. Burrage (New York: Charles Scribner's Sons, 1906), appeared in* The Indian and The White Man, *edited by Wilcomb Washburn (New York: New York University Press, 1964).*

Comprehension

1. What actions did the French take to claim the land Cartier explored?
2. What was the Indian chief's response to the actions of the French?

Critical Thinking

3. Why might the Indians have been glad to be given hatchets and knives?
4. Why might the French have taken two Indians with them?

Primary Sources and Literature

WORKSHEET 5
Literature

Sonia Levitin, *Roanoke: A Novel of the Lost Colony*

Roanoke: A Novel of the Lost Colony, by Sonia Levitin, is a story of the second attempt to build a settlement on Roanoke Island. To narrate the story, Levitin created the character of William Wythers, a sixteen-year-old colonist at Roanoke in 1587. In the passage below, Wythers describes a discussion among the colonists about rebuilding a wall that earlier colonists had constructed around the settlement.

"It's unthinkable to build a settlement without a wall!" cried John Spendlove. "What's to protect our possessions? These flimsy houses?"

"But you see how quickly a fort can crumble," argued John Sampson. "What use is a wall, really?"

"Gentlemen," said Richard Berry stiffly, obviously restraining himself, "never in all history has any land been won and held without a certain show of force. There's absolutely no question. We must rebuild the walls of the fort." . . .

Of all of them, only Ananais leaned first toward one side of the argument, then to the other. "We must keep an open mind," he said. "The Governor feels that if we build a wall it might offend the savages."

"Offend the savages!" cried Chris Cooper, bent over with laughter. "How does one offend a savage?"

"By behaving in a way that seems rude and hostile," Ananais said gravely, and Cooper burst out laughing again.

Thoughtfully Roger Prat spoke up, rising as he did so. "If we wish to reach them," he said, "it seems wrong to first build a wall." . . .

"Go and fetch the Governor," Ananais whispered to me, and with relief I went to find him.

I found him near the beach, speaking to Captain Spicer. . . . When the Governor turned to me, I gave the message. "The Assistants ask that you decide, sir," I concluded, "whether we ought to build a wall first or finish mending the huts. And some," I added, "think we ought not to build a wall at all."

He turned to me, smiling in a half-serious, half-jesting way and asked, "What do you think, William?"

The question brought me up short, as if it were an obstacle in my path. Never before had anyone asked me what I thought. . . .

"A wall," I began, "might make us feel safer at night. And yet, I hear the natives build no walls, and George Howe has told me how it feels to be out—out in the open spaces with only a sky for cover and no walls at all. I think," I said slowly, "if it were possible to build a town without a wall, and to live there without being afraid—it would be a fine thing. John Sampson said that the wall we build to keep them out will also keep us in. And I—I don't think I want to be kept in, sir."

He walked beside me silently, and at last I asked, with a sudden touch of fear, "Have you already made your decision, sir?"

He flashed at me a stern, astonished look, then he laughed heartily. "What you mean, my young friend, is, am I asking you to make the decision?" Again he chuckled, then said, "Yes, I have made the decision, based on a different reason from yours. Though your arguments," he added quickly, "are good ones. We will not build a wall. A wall won't make us stronger than we are. We are stronger than the savages, in many ways, but . . . it's all in the way you look at it. If we could see ourselves not as conquerors, but as guests. . . ." His voice faded, then resumed its strength. "After all, Roanoke is not to be our home. We're moving to Chesapeake next year, and until then we need the friendship of these natives. We have to move into their lives gradually, make ourselves blend into the countryside, so to speak. A wall would only teach them to fear us, and fear always turns into violence in the end."

From Roanoke: A Novel of the Lost Colony *by Sonia Levitin. Copyright © 1973 by Sonia Levitin.*

Critical Thinking

1. What arguments did John Spendlove and Richard Berry use in favor of rebuilding the wall?
2. According to Stevens, what were two possible goals for the Roanoke colony? How would the choice of a goal affect the decision of whether or not to rebuild the wall?
3. What was William's reason for opposing the wall?
4. What did the Governor mean by the statement, "If we could see ourselves not as conquerors, but as guests"?

Connecting History and Literature

Answer one question with a brief essay.

A. What were England's goals in establishing an American colony?
B. What does this excerpt tell you about the colonists' conflicting attitudes toward the Indians?

WORKSHEET 6   Primary Source
Captain John Smith on the Starving Time

Captain John Smith served as leader of the Jamestown colony from 1607 to 1609. Soon after he returned to England, the settlers endured a period of great hardships they called "the starving time." Fifteen years later, Smith wrote *The General History of Virginia*. In it he included this description of Jamestown's most difficult time.

The day before Captain Smith returned for England with the ships [October 4, 1609], Captain Davis arrived in a small pinnace, with some sixteen proper men more. . . . For the savages [Indians] no sooner understood Smith was gone but they all revolted, and did spoil and murder all they encountered. . . .

Now we all found the loss of Captain Smith; yea, his greatest maligners [critics] could now curse his loss. As for corn provision and contribution from the savages, we [now] had nothing but mortal wounds, with clubs and arrows. As for our hogs, hens, goats, sheep, horses, and what lived, our commanders, officers, and savages daily consumed them. Some small proportions sometimes we tasted, till all was devoured; then swords, arms, [fowling] pieces, or anything we traded with the savages, whose cruel fingers were so often imbrued in our blood that what by their cruelty, our Governor's indis-

cretion, and the loss of our ships, of five hundred [persons] within six months after Captain Smith's departure there remained not past sixty men, women, and children, most miserable and poor creatures. And those were preserved for the most part by roots, herbs, acorns, walnuts, berries, now and then a little fish. They that had starch [courage] in these extremities made no small use of it; yea, [they ate] even the very skins of our horses. . . .

This was the time which still to this day [1624] we called the starving time. It were too vile to say, and scarce to be believed, what we endured. But the occasion was our own, for want of providence, industry, and government, and not the barrenness and defect of the country, as is generally supposed.

From The General History of Virginia, New England, and the Summer Isles *(1624), by John Smith.*

Comprehension

1. What happened as soon as Captain Smith left Jamestown?
2. Who got to eat the farm animals that were left?
3. How did the population of Jamestown change in the six months after Captain Smith left?
4. What did the survivors eat to survive?

Critical Thinking

5. On what does Smith blame the starving time? Do you think this is a logical explanation? Why or why not?
6. The starving time occurred after Smith left. Where do you think he got the information for this report? What problems might there be with its accuracy?

WORSHEET 6

Literature

Scott O'Dell, *The Serpent Never Sleeps*

Scott O'Dell's novel *The Serpent Never Sleeps* describes a young woman named Serena Lynn who sails in 1609 from England to the struggling settlement at Jamestown, Virginia. In the passage below, Serena and her fellow passengers finally arrive, after a long and difficult journey, at Jamestown. There they learn first-hand of the conditions within Jamestown's walls.

Tides and shifting winds held us for a day. Then a gentle breeze carried us up the James to a point of land and Jamestown. Below the settlement, tall trees overhung the riverbank. Sailors tied the two ships to the trees, quietly, as if they were tying a pair of horses. Sir Thomas Gates shouted for everyone to line up in an orderly fashion and not to move until he gave the order.

Deliverance fired her cannon. Muskets roared. Bugles sounded. Everyone cheered. Sir Thomas shouted for quiet.

Signaling us to follow, he strode ashore and took a path that led upward to a huddled settlement atop a hillock [small hill]. He held his sword aloft. His scarlet cloak fluttered in the wind and showed a glint of gold braid. Beside him, right and left, drummers beat upon their drums. We followed, singing a sprightly tune. It was a fine display, meant to hearten all the citizens of Jamestown.

But tramping along behind Sir Thomas, I thought it curious that the path we followed was overgrown with weeds and doubly curious that no one from the settlement had come to greet us.

Above me, at the end of the weedgrown path, I caught a glimpse of a stockade with most of the stakes missing, the sagging roof of what was once a fort, a row of ruined huts. Had the settlers left? Had Jamestown been abandoned? If so, Sir Thomas surely would have been told when he talked to those at Fort Comfort.

He came to a halt in front of the stockade. Through the gate, which hung loose on its hinges, stumbled a grizzled old woman, leading a child. Behind her stood a cluster of silent figures. The woman wanted to know if the ships had brought food.

Sir Thomas, though shocked by the desolation that lay around him, by the starving woman and the silent figures, said in a hearty voice, "Two shiploads, good lady. Fish, eggs, turtle meat, strings of smoked birds. We'll spread a grand feast for you ere the sun goes down."

"Now would be the better," the old woman said. "A little now. Some of us will not be here when the sun goes down."

"So now it is," said Sir Thomas in the same hearty voice, and sent a bevy of guards headlong to the ships.

The child wandered over and grasped the hem of my skirt. She had blue eyes and corn-colored hair that needed combing.

"What name do you have?" I asked her. "Humility," she said. "And my mother's name is Humility, too."

"It's a pretty name. How nice. Where is your mother?"

"In heaven," the child said. "My father is in heaven, too. I will see them soon. . . ."

Our people gazed at the ruined fort and the tumbled barricade and the starving. They must have wished, all of them except our leaders and the Reverend Bucke, that they were back in the soft airs of Bermuda, among the palm trees and the blue water and bounteous shoals of food, just for the taking. Their groans were tight-lipped and silent, but I heard them nonetheless.

Barrels of smoked pork were trundled up the hill. Governor Gates had them opened for all to see, but the starving people hung back.

"Step up, my friends," he said in his stentorian voice. "There are more barrels of pork, barrels of fish, and birds laid down in fat awaiting you."

A man standing beside the governor said, "It's been a terrible time. We've had scarce a handful of corn each day. This, for weeks now. The smell of food, the mere sight of it, must make them ill as it does me. Bear with us, I pray you. We'll soon get our stomachs back."

The man, I learned, was Sir George Percy. He had been president of the colony since the day Captain Smith was badly burned in a fire and forced to return to England.

The colony had fared well under Smith's guidance. . . . He had frowned on laziness. Those who did not work did not eat. Those who disobeyed orders were punished. He went boldly among the Indians, often alone, threatening them if himself threatened, carrying out his threats if need be.

But no more than sixty of some five hundred settlers had survived the past six months. "A deathly winter," Sir George Percy said as he stood gazing at the food spread out upon the grass, still unable to touch it.

"We called it 'the Starving Time.' We ventured outside the fort only to bury our dead, but only at night in shallow graves, for the earth was frozen and we feared death from savage arrows. Inside the fort stalked famine and pestilence. Huts of the dead and pickets from the stockade were burned for firewood. So great was the famine that an Indian we managed to slay was consumed. One amongst our starving slew his wife and was secretly eating her when discovered. Truly, a Starving Time. My friends, if you had not come at this fateful hour, we all would have been dead within the week."

From The Serpent Never Sleeps *by Scott O'Dell. Copyright © 1987 by Scott O'Dell, published by Houghton Mifflin Company.*

Critical Thinking

1. Contrast the appearance of the new arrivals with that of the Jamestown settlers.
2. What did the old woman mean when she told Sir Thomas that "some of us will not be here when the sun goes down"?
3. Why did the Jamestown settlers not want to eat the food brought to them right away?

Connecting History and Literature

Answer one question with a brief essay.

A. Why were Jamestown's settlers in such poor health?
B. Explain why the success of England's North American colonies depended on a strong English navy.

WORKSHEET 7
A Sermon by Jonathan Edwards

"Sinners in the Hands of an Angry God" was the title of this sermon, Edwards's most famous. He delivered it in Enfield, Connecticut, on July 8, 1741. The sermon's emotional passion reflects the intense feelings of the Great Awakening.

The bow of God's wrath is bent, and the arrow made ready on the string, and justice bends the arrow at your heart, and strains the bow, and it is nothing but the mere pleasure of God, and that of an angry God, without any promise or obligation at all, that keeps the arrow one moment from being made drunk with your blood. Thus all you that never passed under a great change of heart, by the mighty power of the Spirit of God upon your souls; all you that were never born again, and made new creatures, and raised from being dead in sin, to a state of new, and before altogether unexperienced light and life, are in the hands of an angry God. However you may have reformed your life in many things, and may have had religious affections, and may keep up a form of religion in your families and closets, and in the house of God, it is nothing but his mere pleasure that keeps you from being this moment swallowed up in everlasting destruction. However unconvinced you may now be of the truth of what you hear, by and by you will be fully convinced of it. . . .

The God that holds you over the pit of hell, much as one holds a spider, or some loathsome insect over the fire, abhors you, and is dreadfully provoked: his wrath towards you burns like fire; he looks upon you as worthy of nothing else, but to be cast into the fire; he is of purer eyes than to bear to have you in his sight; you are ten thousand times more abominable in his eyes, than the most hateful venomous serpent is in ours. You have offended him infinitely more than ever a stubborn rebel did his prince; and yet it is nothing but his hand that holds you from falling into the fire every moment. . . .

O sinner! Consider the fearful danger you are in: it is a great furnace of wrath, a wide and bottomless pit, full of the fire of wrath, that you are held over in the hand of that God, whose wrath is provoked and incensed as much against you, as against many of the damned in hell. You hang by a slender thread, with the flames of divine wrath flashing about it, and ready every moment to singe it, and burn it asunder; and you have no interest in any Mediator, and nothing to lay hold of to save yourself, nothing to keep off the flames of wrath, nothing of your own, nothing that you ever have done, nothing that you can do, to induce God to spare you one moment.

"Sinners in the Hands of an Angry God" reprinted in American Testament: Fifty Great Documents in American History *(American Heritage, 1971).*

Comprehension

1. According to Edwards, what force prevents his listeners from being condemned to hell?
2. Are religious persons safe from damnation, according to Edwards?
3. What is God's attitude toward the listeners, according to Edwards?

Critical Thinking

4. What did Edwards mean by the phrase "great change of heart" in the first paragraph?
5. How do you think this sermon affected its listeners?

WORSHEET 7 Benjamin Franklin's Almanac

WORKSHEET 7 Benjamin Franklin's Almanac   **Literature**

In 1733, Benjamin Franklin began printing annually a small pamphlet called *Poor Richard's Almanack.* In an excerpt from one of these pamphlets, a fictitious Father Abraham gives advice on managing work and leisure.

. . . *Dost thou love Life, then do not squander Time, for that's the Stuff Life is made of,* as Poor Richard says . . . . If Time be of all Things the most precious, *wasting Time* must be . . . *the greatest Prodigality,* since . . . *Lost Time is never found again;* and what we call *Time-enough, always proves little enough.* Let us then be up and be doing, and doing to the Purpose; so by Diligence shall we do more with less Perplexity. *Sloth makes all Things difficult, but Industry all easy,* as Poor Richard says; and *He that riseth late, must trot all Day.* . . . While . . . *Early to Bed, and early to rise, makes a Man healthy, wealthy and wise.* . . .

Industry need not wish, as Poor Richard says and He that lives upon Hope will die fasting. . . . If we are industrious we shall never starve; for, as Poor Richard says, *At the working Man's House Hunger looks in, but dares not enter.* Nor will the Bailiff nor the Constable enter, for *Industry pays Debts, while Despair encreaseth them,* says Poor Richard. . . . *Diligence is the Mother of Good luck . . .* , and *God gives all Things to Industry.* . . .

Methinks I hear some of you say, *Must a Man afford himself no Leisure?* I will tell thee, my Friend, what Poor Richard says, *Employ thy Time well if thou meanest to gain Leisure;* and, *since thou art not sure of a Minute, throw not away an Hour.* Leisure, is Time for doing something useful; this Leisure the diligent Man will obtain, but the lazy Man never; so that, as Poor Richard says, a *Life of Leisure and a Life of Laziness are two Things.*

From "Father Abrahams Speech" in the 1757 edition of Poor Richard's Almanack, by Benjamin Franklin. Quoted in An American Primer, *edited by Daniel J. Boorstin (The University of Chicago Press, 1966).*

Critical Thinking

1. What did Franklin say was most important, or precious, in life? Why?
2. What were Franklin's views on work, or "industry"? From which evils would it protect us?
3. What did Franklin think about leisure?

Connecting History and Literature

Answer one question with a brief essay

A. Do you agree with Franklin's ideas? Write a short essay explaining why or why not.
B. How does Franklin's advice reflect the economic conditions in the American colonies?

WORKSHEET 8 Franklin Describes Braddock's Defeat   **Primary Source**

In 1755 Benjamin Franklin organized teams of wagons and horses to help the British army attack the French in western Pennsylvania. Years later in his autobiography he wrote this passage about General Braddock.

In conversation with him one day he was giving me some account of his intended progress. "After taking Fort Duquesne," says he, "I am to proceed to Niagara; and, having taken that, to Frontenac, if the season will allow time, and I suppose it will, for Duquesne can hardly detain me above three or four days; and then I see nothing that can obstruct my march to Niagara." Having before revolved in my mind the long line his army must make in their march . . . and also what I had read of a former defeat of fifteen hundred French, who invaded the Iroquois country, I had conceived some doubts and some fears for the event of the campaign. But I ventured only to say: "To be sure, sir, if you arrive well before Duquesne with these fine troops . . . that place . . . can probably make but a short resistance. The only danger I apprehend of obstruction to your march is from ambuscades [ambushes] of Indians . . . and the slender line, near four miles long, which your army must make, may expose it to be attacked by surprise in its flanks, and to be cut like a thread into several pieces, which, from their distance, cannot come up in time to support each other."

He smiled at my ignorance, and replied: "These savages may, indeed, be a formidable enemy to your raw American militia, but upon the King's regular and disciplined troops, sir, it is impossible they should make any impression." I was conscious of an impropriety in my disputing with a military man in matters of his profession, and said no more. The enemy, however, did not take the advantage of his army which I apprehended its long line of march exposed it to, but let it advance . . . till . . . when more in a body . . . and in a more open part of the woods than any it had passed, attacked its advance guard by heavy fire from behind trees and bushes, which was the first intelligence the general had of an enemy's being near him. This guard being disordered, the general hurried the troops up to their assistance, which was done in great confusion, through wagons, baggage, and cattle, and presently the fire came upon their flank. The officers, being on horseback, were more easily distinguished, picked out as marks, and fell very fast; and the soldiers were crowded together in a huddle, having or hearing no orders, and standing to be shot at till two-thirds of them were killed; and then, being seized with a panic, the whole fled with precipitation. . . . This whole transaction gave us Americans the first suspicion that our exalted ideas of the prowess of British regulars had not been well founded.

From The Autobiography of Benjamin Franklin, *by Benjamin Franklin, originally published in 1793.*

Comprehension

1. What was Braddock's attitude before setting off to fight?
2. What did Franklin fear would happen to Braddock's troops?
3. How did the enemy attack the British soldiers?
4. What was the outcome of the battle?

Critical Thinking

5. Franklin began writing his autobiography in 1771 and continued through the American Revolution until 1789. How might his view of Braddock have changed over this period?

WORSHEET 8 Kenneth Roberts, *Northwest Passage*   **Literature**

Kenneth Roberts' exciting historical novels of colonial life gained him a wide readership. In *Northwest Passage,* set mainly in New York State, Roberts uses the French and Indian War as a backdrop. A high-spirited young artist named Langdon Towne has been thrown out of Harvard College. He signs on with the forces of Robert Rogers, who has vowed to wipe out the Indian village of St. Francis in French Canada. In the following passage, "Rogers' Rangers" approach the village.

When we had carried the boats a hundred yards to dry earth and packed their lockers with provisions we'd use after our return, we hid them beneath screens of pine. I had expected Canada to be cold, but the marshy forest steamed with a breathless sultry heat. Clouds of mosquitoes rose from the swamp whining and singing about our heads. With every breath, we drew them into our throats, and coughed and spat mosquitoes. . . .

No sooner were the boats hidden than he [Rogers] paraded us. Possessed of a demon of impatience, he was up and down our lines and everywhere, urging us to move faster, and the same time strapping on his knapsack and blanket, hanging his belt with hatchet and corn-meal bag. He hovered around us like a persistent bee, tweaking [twisting] knapsack straps, shaking powderhorns, looking at moccasins.

To me he said, to be noted in my orderly book, "I'm leaving two Indians on the high land to watch the boats—Lieutenant Solomon and Konkapot. They'll stay here till we come back, unless the French find the boats. In that case Solomon and Konkapot'll come after us to bring the report."

As the men jostled into position, fastening the last of their equipment to their belts, Sergeant Bradley hustled me into place behind Ogden and beside Jesse Beacham. Captain Jacobs and eight of his Stockbridge Indians, stripped to the waist and covered with grease and paint, ran ahead to act as advance scouts and stopped at the end of the high land to look back at us.

"Follow the lake shore to the northeastern tip of Missisquoi Bay," Rogers called up and down the lines. "That's our meeting place in case we have to scatter. We'll strike inland there. Until we're out of the swamps, we'll march abreast."

He looked from one end of his tiny army to the other, and I saw a hint of a dubious smile appear upon his heavy lips, as if we were only partly to his liking. From neck to thigh we were hung with clumsy equipment. Our labors in the heat and dampness had given us a sweaty and raffish [careless] look, and splashed us with mud and water; and some had even rubbed themselves with mud to protect themselves from mosquitoes. No wonder Rogers wore that dubious smile.

The advance guard of Indians ranged forward, vanished, and then the long advance of the rest of us began. We struck wet ground at once, of course, and plodded into it. I hoped that we might pass it soon, and that my breeches, unlike poor Bradley's, might remain upon me. Through the dense trees, to our left, we caught glimpses of blue Missisquoi Bay, as cool and tranquil as we were hot and uncomfortable. . . .

When, at dusk, we reached a dry ridge, he gave the word to camp for the night. The straps of my blanket and knapsack had cut me like iron bands, and to sit down was torture, but to get up was worse.

I stood there watching Rogers; wondering how he did it. He had Bradley and Lieutenant Farrington, and with their help had hoisted himself to the lower branches of a tall spruce.

He went up it like a big squirrel, almost to the top, and clung there, peering back along our route. There was nothing, no exertion or hardship, he couldn't bear and be fresh at the end of it.

Through the dull fatigue that numbed me, his thick voice, mumbling to Ogden, was the last thing I heard at night, and it was that same thick voice that, in the morning, awakened me to a wet blanket and aching joints.

I can hear him now, shouting to the offi-cers: "Get 'em up! They got ten minutes to get started! Get 'em up! Get 'em up!"

From Northwest Passage *by Kenneth Roberts. Copyright © 1936, 1937 by Kenneth Roberts, published by Doubleday.*

Critical Thinking

1. What difficulties did the men encounter as they approach the enemy village?
2. Why did Rogers wear a "dubious smile"?
3. How did the narrator regard Rogers?

Connecting History and Literature

Answer one question with a brief essay.

A. Although Rogers' force was on its way to attack an Indian village, he was accompanied by Indians as well. Explain why this was so.
B. What were the causes and results of the French and Indian War?

WORKSHEET 9 Resolutions of the Stamp Act Congress   **Primary Source**

Although only nine colonies sent delegates to the Stamp Act Congress, the remaining four colonies did not oppose the Congress's goals. One of these colonies, New Hampshire, approved the resolutions of the Stamp Act Congress after they were written. The three remaining colonies— Virginia, North Carolina, and Georgia—had been prevented from electing delegates by their royal governors. The strongest issue of debate among the 27 delegates was whether to modify the rebellious tone of the resolutions. Below are some of the significant resolutions of the Stamp Act Congress.

The members of this Congress . . . esteem it our indispensable duty to make the following declarations of our humble opinion, respecting the most essential rights and liberties of the colonists, and of the grievances under which they labour, by reason of several late Acts of Parliament.

I. That His Majesty's subjects in these colonies, owe the same allegiance to the Crown of Great Britain, that is owing from his subjects born within the realm, and all due subordination to that august body the Parliament of Great Britain.

II. That His Majesty's liege subjects in these colonies, are entitled to all the inherent rights and liberties of his natural born subjects within the kingdom of Great-Britain.

III. That it is inseparably essential to the freedom of a people, and the undoubted right of Englishmen, that no taxes be imposed on them, but with their own consent, given personally, or by their representatives.

IV. That the people of these colonies are not, and from their local circumstances cannot be, represented in the House of Commons in Great-Britain.

V. That the only representatives of the people of these colonies, are persons chosen therein by themselves, and that no taxes ever have been, or can be constitutionally imposed on them, but by their respective legislatures. . . .

VIII. That the late Act of Parliament, entitled, *An Act for granting and applying certain Stamp Duties, and other Duties, in the British colonies and plantations in America, etc.,* by imposing taxes on the inhabitants of these Colonies . . . [has] a manifest tendency to subvert the rights and liberties of the colonists. . . .

XI. That the restrictions imposed by several late Acts of Parliament, on the trade of these colonies, will render them unable to purchase the manufactures of Great-Britain. . . .

Lastly, That it is the indispensable duty of these colonies . . . to endeavour by a loyal and dutiful address to his Majesty, and humble applications to both Houses of Parliament, to procure the repeal of the Act for granting and applying certain stamp duties. . . .

From Resolutions of the Stamp Act Congress, in Great Issues in American History, Vol. I *ed. by Richard Hofstadter (New York: Vintage, 1958).*

Comprehension

1. What right of all Englishmen did the colonists claim for themselves?
2. What reason did the colonists give for the unconstitutionality of Parliament imposing a tax upon them?

Critical Thinking

3. Which resolution contained the threat of a boycott? Explain.
4. Which resolution was designed to ease the fears of the king and Parliament?

WORSHEET 9 Erick Berry, *Sybil Ludington's Ride* **Literature**

The American Revolution was fought by famous soldiers like George Washington and by ordinary people as well. Many of these unknown soldiers were part-time fighters—militiamen—who had to be called together to fight a battle. How were these soldiers notified that they were needed when there was no telephone, radio, or television? Who brought the message to them? In Erick Berry's *Sybil Ludington's Ride,* 16-year-old Sybil Ludington makes a nearly 40-mile journey on horseback to deliver the message that "the British are coming."

The pitch-black night closed down like a shutter. There followed a slight struggle. For Star didn't approve of the cold wet night and wanted to return to the comfort of his stable; at least that was what Sybil hoped. But in the darkness it was quite possible she was trying to ride him through the thick trunk of the butternut tree, and to that he quite naturally objected.

No, there was a deeper dark against the black, the tree trunk. And a moment after, Star stumbled into the deep ruts of the road. Left or right? Left of course; the horse protesting only because he felt that any road was the wrong road on a night like this.

The roar of the millstream came clear above the drumming of the rain, and there on the right bulked the shape of the mill.

Jake Hunter's there on the right, she was sure of it. And here was the turn-in. There was a light too, in the kitchen. But had she really come so short a distance? For this wasn't Jake's after all, it was only the Gillettes'.

She rode Star up to the window—it was no matter that he tramped Mrs. Gillette's yarbs [herbs]—and hammered noisily on the shutter with her fist. The window swung open.

"Father sent me to carry warning," she began politely, as though she were inviting the woman to supper at the Ludingtons'.

"You, gal, at this time of night!" said Mrs. Gillette. "Is aught [anything] wrong? Hitch, and come right in."

Sybil took a deep breath and tried again, this time in a firmer tone. "The British are burning Danbury. Tell Mr. Gillette that the troops are to muster immediately. Women and children to bundle up their valuables and be ready to drive off livestock, if the redcoats come this way. And please spread word to your neighbors." That was her full message. She wheeled Star and headed him down the road. She hoped the woman would believe her and take warning.

Only a short ride—Star more willing now—to the Hunters'. The house was dark; could she afford time to waken them? Oh, she must, for he was a corporal in the militia and mighty dependable. But she would remember that the message she brought was military. She reined up, hammered lustily at the shutter, and shouted, "Rouse! Rouse! The British are burning Danbury!" There would be no need here to explain what that meant, what it meant to the whole countryside.

A head came out of a window, and Jake's voice said almost placidly, "That'll mean a mustering."

"And please to tell your neighbors." . . .

Two more households were wakened without difficulty and one even remembered to thank her. Then she encountered what threatened to be a failure. Susannah Oppershore utterly refused to waken her deaf husband. "There's been a sight too many musterin's," she snapped at Sybil through the half-open window. "And a man's got his duty by his wife and farm. Likely enough it's a false alarm, like all the others."

Disgusted, furious with the woman's selfishness, scarce able to believe anyone could be so shortsighted, Sybil tried again.

"But this time the British are at Danbury. We need every soldier—"

"Let the Danbury folk fight them, then," snapped the woman. "And you go right home and quit pesterin' folks."

Sybil, glancing anxiously along the road, desperate to be off again, noted how much clearer the bare trees showed against the sky. What was that glow? Surely not moonrise, with all this rain. She turned to the woman, about to close her window.

"If you don't believe me, ma'am," she said, "look out at the sky there. 'Tis Danbury burning. You can see the glare of it on the clouds. Like enough the redcoats are marching this way even now.

"The redcoats comin' this way?" The woman's anger changed suddenly to fear. She turned to shout back into the house, "Timothy! You there, Timothy! D'you want us all to be burned in our beds? . . ."

Sybil missed the rest of it.

At Carmel settlement she paused to summon only three; one offered to ride on with her. The thought of having a human companion on the lonely dark road was tempting, so tempting. But she told him the route she was taking, the road to the lake, and begged him to spread the alarm east along the highroad. Before she was out of the settlement she heard the raucous [rough-sounding] clamor of the village bell; it bore her reassuring company for nigh [nearly] a mile.

Then came a long and cheerless stretch. The yearling's first burst of energy and her own excitement were fading into a dull, dogged purpose. She tried to sing against the pelting rain. Star pricked up his ears and seemed to move more cheerfully. . . .

In front of her, for mile after dark mile, lay a sleeping, defenseless countryside. Behind her, kindled by her message, lights had sprung up, hearthfires had been raked to a blaze, lanterns carried at a run to barns, to neighbors lying off the route. Voices called to voices, people were dressing, women packing in haste, men shouting for their arms, for musket and powder horn and bullet bag,

and saddling or hasting away on foot. Children, bundled still sleeping from their cots, or the older ones sent on errands, given tasks; this one to help grandmother, that one to catch up the hens in readiness for flight, another to bury the pewter in the garden— she could imagine a hundred such happenings.

But before her, nothing but darkness, sleep, unreadiness. No, for there was a glow ahead, more than a houselight. A glow of a firelight through the trees. Soldiers, mustering, perhaps, to march to the Ludingtons', had kindled a small blaze? But it seemed unlikely.

Whoever they were they must be told. She turned Star off the road, headed him in the direction of the bonfire, and left it to him to thread his way between the rocks and undergrowth.

She could see six men or thereabouts. And horses. And, yes, firearms were propped beside the seated men as they warmed themselves at the blaze.

But no man with farming to do would be awake and camped out in the open at this time of night, and the British could scarcely have reached here as yet. But all the same it was relief to see that the men wore no colored uniform. Which made it likely they were militia.

She was near enough now to shout. And was just about to, when a stone turned under Star's hoof and went rattling down a short slope. A man sprang up from the fireside and grabbed his musket.

Sybil jerked tight the rein. The appetizing odor of roast mutton had reached her. And there, slowly turning on a greenwood spit beside the fire, was the best part of a stolen sheep.

Not British, not militia, these men. They were thieves and robbers, cowboys or skinners [guerrillas].

Desperately she turned the yearling; and, eyes blinded by the firelight, headed him back into the darkness.

A chorus of shouts. The cutthroats were after her.

There was no knowing what these outlaws

would do if they caught her. And if they captured her, who would spread the alarm? Her safety, Star's safety, was nothing beside the safety of the whole countryside.

She had a hundred paces' start. Add a few moments while the cutthroats were catching and saddling their horses. If only she could gallop, gallop, lose herself in the darkness.

But here under the thick trees there was no chance even of picking her direction. And at every panic attempt to make for the road, boulders, a stream bed, giant tree trunks, headed her off. Star stumbled and slipped at a scrambling walk. . . .

Twice the yearling nearly fell and all but pitched her off in his efforts to recover balance. She dismounted and tried to lead him; that might be easier for Star, but it was harder, a heap harder, for Sybil. Slipping and sliding over wet leaves, wedging a foot between rocks, blundering into tree trunks, she could have cried with sheer fatigue and vexation. And every moment of delay might be bringing the enemy closer, closer; while militiamen, badly needed, slumbered in their homes.

Suddenly, from nearby, came a man's voice. "Who's that?"

One of the cattle stealers, no doubt, thinking he had come across a comrade. She could see the darker shadow in the dimness, and he must be able to see her, for the summons came again.

And more sharply this time. "Who's there?"

She stretched out an arm, as though with a pistol. "Stand, or I fire!"

"Holy Moses!" in tones of surprise. "That ain't you, Sybil Ludington? It's me, Zeke Cowper, that you roused a while since. I'm cuttin' cross-lots [taking a short cut] to the other road, to pass on your warning. But cripes above, this is no place for you to be ridin'."

Sybil could have burst into tears with sheer relief. But fearful that his loud, cheerful voice might betray them, she begged him to be quiet and whispered her news of the skinners' camp.

"Once the war's won we'll hang 'em all, skinners and cowboys alike," he rumbled angrily. "But you let me lead your horse and you follow. It's only a step across here to the next road."

Zeke's idea of a "step" was a giant's stride, but they did reach the road at last, a road that lay east of the one she had been following. "Just head north, for Ben Hasbrouck's place," he advised her as he helped her back into the saddle. "Then turn east for Stormville; Ben'll show you." And promised, if he arrived first, to tell her father that, so far, all was well.

Frightened she was now, and she would admit as much, after that meeting with the skinners. It called for all the courage she could lay hand on to ride in off the road and rouse the next farm. At Ben Hasbrouck's, at the turn of the road, they set her on her new direction, and surprised her by telling her it was no later than midnight, when she had thought the dawn itself must be close. But more than half her ride was over; Star, who had gone lame for a while, had only caught a stone in his hoof, and once she had that out, he was striding out as gallantly as before. Never, as long as she lived, would she forget how brave, how helpful he was. If ever there was a good patriot, it was Star this night. Heavens, how tired she was! Every muscle ached, and legs and even arms were bruised from floundering around among those rocks. But strangely enough she had never been happier in her life, though she didn't know it herself till she found herself singing.

A mile or so later and with a good hour's ride still ahead of her, her troubles were already over; someone riding from the opposite direction had already spread the alarm. First there were lighted houses; then there were armed men, in twos and threes, striding on grimly to muster for defense, to fight for freedom. They gave her a shout and some gave her a cheer as Star, spurred on by excitement, galloped past. Soon she was traveling among a little group of horsemen, men who had come from farther west. The group included a woman riding with her husband so she could lead back the much needed team after he joined his regiment.

The procession grew till there must have been a score [twenty] or more, pounding the road like a troop of cavalry. Inspired by the other horses, excited perhaps by the two or three lanterns, Star threw up his head proudly and stretched his pace. South through Stormville, where a blacksmith's apprentice was still loudly pounding on a wagon tire to spread the alarm, southeast down a road that grew more and more familiar, they swung.

Into the Ludington lane, down past the mill, which had been flung open to shelter those who couldn't squeeze into either house or barn. Constant scurrying to and fro, the rumble of men's voices, the sharp bark of orders from officers: Sybil had seen and heard it all before, but this time she was a part of it. She had received her orders and carried them out like a soldier.

At the gate someone took Star and offered to stable him. Reluctantly she surrendered him. 'Twas like giving up part of herself. "Best rub him down," said Sybil. "He's done a long ride." The gathering at the house door made way for her.

"Here she is, Colonel. Here's your aide, sir." And Father himself threw down his quill and, in full regimentals [uniform], rose from the table to greet her and hear her report, just as he would for a soldier. This surely was the proudest moment of her life.

From Sybil Ludington's Ride *by Erick Berry. Copyright © 1952 by Erick Berry. Reprinted by permission of William K.H. Coxe.*

Critical Thinking

1. What was Sybil's mission?
2. What dangers did she face along the way?
3. What was Sybil's mood at the end of the ride?

Connecting History and Literature

Answer one question with a brief essay.

A. When and why had colonists begun organizing militias?
B. What does this excerpt tell you about the difficulty the British would face in resisting American independence?

WORKSHEET 10
The Northwest Ordinance of 1787

Primary Source

Early settlement south of the Ohio River and east of the Mississippi was disorganized. Many claims, counterclaims, and lawsuits resulted. By contrast, the Northwest Ordinance tried to settle the land north of the Ohio River in a more organized fashion.

Sec 3. Be it ordained by the authority aforesaid, That there shall be appointed, from time to time, by Congress, a governor, whose commission shall continue in force for the term of three years. . . .

Sec. 4. There shall be appointed . . . by Congress, a secretary, whose commission shall continue in force for four years. . . . There shall also be appointed a court, to consist of three judges . . . who shall have a common-law jurisdiction. . . .

Sec. 9. So soon as there shall be five thousand free male inhabitants, of full age, in the district, upon giving proof thereof to the governor, they shall receive authority . . . to elect representatives from their counties or townships, to represent them in the general assembly. . . .

Sec. 14. It is hereby ordained and declared . . . that the following articles shall be considered as articles of compact between the original states and the people and states in the said territory. . . .

Article I
No person . . . shall ever be molested on account of his mode of worship, or religious sentiments, in the said territory.

Article II
The inhabitants of the said territory shall always be entitled to the benefits of the writs of habeas corpus and of the trial by jury. . . .

Article III
Religion, morality, and knowledge being necessary to good government and the happiness of mankind, schools and the means of education shall forever be encouraged. The utmost good faith shall always be observed toward the Indians; their lands and property shall never be taken from them without their consent. . . .

Article VI
There shall be neither slavery nor involuntary servitude in the said territory. . . . Provided always, That any person escaping into the same, from whom labor or service is lawfully claimed in any one of the original states, such fugitive may be lawfully reclaimed, and conveyed to the person claiming his or her labor or service as aforesaid. . . .

Northwest Ordinance of 1787, *as printed in* Sources of the American Republic, *Vol. I, compiled by Marvin Meyers Alexander Kern, and John G. Cawelti (Chicago: Scott Foresman, 1960).*

Comprehension

1. What was the structure of government in a territory?
2. What requirements did the Northwest Ordinance establish for a territory to form a representative assembly?
3. What policy toward the Indians is found in the Northwest Ordinance? Cite the article in which this policy is stated.
4. Which article deals with legal rights of citizens?

Critical Thinking

5. How did Article VI discourage slaves from fleeing to the territories in search of freedom?

WORKSHEET 10
Scott O'Dell, *Sarah Bishop*

Sarah Bishop describes the experiences of a young girl named Sarah Bishop during the Revolutionary War. Sarah lives on a farm on Long Island, New York, with her father, a Loyalist, and her brother, Chad. In the passage below, Sarah and her father stand by their house as shots come from a nearby mill.

"Why is Quarme shooting at us?" I asked.

"He's not shooting at us," my father said. "He's shooting in our direction. Just to remind us."

"Of what?"

"That he owns a new firelock [gun]. That he's for the revolution. That he's hot to run King George and all his men out of the country. And that he knows we are against the revolution and for King George."

Another bullet went over, no closer than the others, but it seemed closer. I thought it would be a good idea if we got ourselves in the house until Quarme was through shooting, but my father didn't move. He was a tall man with a gaunt [thin] face and a long, stubborn chin, which he rubbed when he was thinking hard.

He stood there rubbing his chin until the shooting stopped. Then he went off to the house without saying a word. . . .

The day was streaming hot, even for August; even the breeze from the sea was hot. So I started the fire in the firebox outside, where it was cooler than inside the house, and mixed up some cakes, using the fish Chad had caught, red-eared corn we had raised and the fresh milk.

Father came in when he couldn't see to work any longer; Chad was late from the tavern.

Father was worried. "He's been coming late the last week."

"The tavern is full, Chad says, running over with travelers from everywhere."

"Mostly from Boston," Father said. "They ran Admiral Howe out of the city, clean up to Halifax, but some of the wiser ones figure that he'll return one of these days soon, this time with the whole British navy in back of him, and make mincemeat out of all the so-called patriots."

Father was bitter about the rebellion. He talked a lot about it and brooded over it when he wasn't talking. We had a drawing of King George with his crown on and a long jeweled robe. It hung on the wall above my father's bed, and every morning and evening he would stand stiff in front of the picture and raise his hand and salute like a soldier, although he had never been one in his life nor ever planned to be.

That was up to three weeks ago, before the picture disappeared. Father blamed Chad for taking it down. When Chad said he hadn't and swore on the Bible, Father still didn't believe him. They didn't speak to each other for a whole day. Then my brother finally admitted that he had put the picture of King George in the fire.

"I've been learning things up at the tavern," Chad said. "For one thing, it's a good idea to keep your mouth shut about the feelings you have."

"A man should do what he wants in his own home," Father said. "Hang a picture of the devil on the wall, if he wants to."

"If one of the patriots happened to walk in here and see a picture of King George sitting up there on the wall, it would be all over the countryside by next day noon."

"Also a man should stand up for what he thinks, not mince around."

"That's what old man Somers over in Hempstead tried to do. He called John Adams a windbag. The patriot boys heard about it and went over and burned his pigsty. They told him that unless he minded his ways, they'd come back and burn his barn."

Father gave Chad a sharp look. "You're not getting scared? You're not changing over, are you? I'm not going to wake up one morning to find you've joined the Skinners."

The Skinners were gangs of young men who went around burning people's property and wanted to hang King George from the nearest tree. I knew that Chad had several friends who belonged to the Skinners. Likewise, that he was not so strong against the rebellion as Father was. In fact, he had told me once that he didn't believe in being taxed by a king who lived thousands of miles away.

I put the fishcakes on the trestle with a bowl of tomato sauce and lit the lamp.

Father sat down and said grace. Then he said to Chad, "You're sure you are just being cautious, not changing your mind about the war?"

Chad put a whole fishcake in his mouth and was silent. . . .

"No, just being sensible," Chad said, talking around the fishcake. "I'm trying to keep out of trouble with the Skinners and the rest of the patriots."

It was quiet for a while. Then from the direction of Purdy's mill came a bang, and after a moment a whistling sound, like a long sigh, passed over the house.

Chad got up and turned out the lamp and we sat in the dark.

From Sarah Bishop *by Scott O'Dell. Copyright © 1980 by Scott O'Dell, published by Houghton Mifflin Company.*

Critical Thinking

1. Why did Chad burn the king's portrait?
2. What was his father's reaction?
3. How are the Patriots presented?
4. How did the conflict between Patriots and Loyalists affect Sarah's family?

Connecting History and Literature

Answer one question with a brief essay.

A. In what way was the American Revolution a civil war?
B. How would divisions among Americans have hurt the Patriot cause?

WORSHEET 11
Arguments for a Bill of Rights

Primary Source

Both Patrick Henry, an Antifederalist, and James Madison, a Federalist, supported a bill of rights, but for quite different reasons.

Patrick Henry's Speech Before the Ratifying Convention, June 5, 1788

I need not take much pains to show, that the principles of this system [the Constitution] are extremely dangerous. . . .

Here is a revolution as radical as that which separated us from Great Britain. The rights of conscience, trial by jury, liberty of the press, all pretensions [claims] to human rights and privileges, are rendered insecure if not lost, by this change. . . . Is this tame relinquishment of rights worthy of freemen?

It is said eight States have adopted this plan. I declare that if twelve States and a half had adopted it, I would . . . reject it.

You are not to inquire how your trade may be increased, nor how you are to become a great and powerful people, but how your liberties can be secured; for liberty ought to be the direct end of your government.

James Madison's Letter to Thomas Jefferson, October 17, 1788

My own opinion has always been in favor of a bill of rights. . . . At the same time I have never . . . been anxious to supply it . . . for any other reason than that it is anxiously desired by others. . . .

I have not viewed it in an important light . . . because . . . the rights in question are reserved by the manner in which the federal powers are granted . . . [and] because experience proves the inefficiency of a bill of rights on those occasions when its control is most needed. . . . Wherever the real power in a Government lies, there is the danger of oppression. In our Governments the real power lies in the majority of the Community. . . .

Altho . . . the danger of oppression lies in the interested majorities of the people rather than in usurped acts of the Government, yet there may be occasions on which the evil may spring from the latter source; and on such, a bill of rights will be a good ground for an appeal to the sense of the community. . . . It is a melancholy [sad] reflection that liberty should be equally exposed to danger whether the Government have too much or too little power. . . .

First passage adapted from Jonathan Elliot, Debates, Resolutions, and Other Proceedings in Convention on the Adoption of the Federal Constitution *(1827-1836). Second passage quoted in* The Complete Madison, His Basic Writings, *edited by Saul K. Padover (Harper & Brothers Publishers, 1973).*

Comprehension

1. Why did Patrick Henry want a bill of rights added to the Constitution?
2. What are two reasons given by Madison for adding a bill of rights to the Constitution?
3. Madison said that the threat to individual rights came from the source of power in a government. At that time, who held the power in government, according to Madison?

Critical Thinking

4. Explain what Madison meant by his remark that liberty was endangered as much by a weak government as by a strong government.

WORKSHEET 11
Catherine Drinker Bowen, *Miracle at Philadelphia*

Literature

In *Miracle at Philadelphia,* written in 1966, historian Catherine Drinker Bowen retells the events surrounding the writing and ratification of the Constitution. The following selection describes the battle between Federalists and Antifederalists at the Virginia ratifying convention, attended by such famous names as James Madison, James Monroe, Patrick Henry, John Marshall, and Edmund Randolph.

While New Hampshire met and adjourned and delayed, Virginia was holding her convention at Richmond, in the new Academy on Shockoe Hill. The country looked to the Old Dominion [Virginia], wondering which way she would go. Virginia's territory reached to the Mississippi; it included the District of Kentucky and West Virginia. Her population was a fifth of the population of the entire Union. Should Virginia ratify, she would be the ninth state, or so she thought; New Hampshire's final vote was still three weeks away. If Virginia refused, New York, North Carolina and Rhode Island would doubtless follow her lead.

This was to be the ablest of all the ratification conventions and the best prepared, a gathering studded with stars, with names and faces known throughout the state and beyond—well-speaking gentlemen on both sides, well-dressed, wellborn. More than a fourth were military men. . . . They had fought the British, they had fought the Indians, and in political conviction they were ranged on both sides. . . .

Chief among Antifederalists was Patrick Henry, tall, thin, stooped, and at fifty-two looking on himself as aged and broken in health. He wore spectacles, concealed his reddish-brown hair by a brown wig, not too well-fitting. His blue eye was still keen, his long face alive with feeling; the old magic waited to be called up at will. "I fear that overwhelming torrent, Patrick Henry," wrote General Knox to Rufus King when the convention was well under way.

From the first day, Henry was the nerve center of the room. "The Henryites," they called his followers. Every Federalist came girded [prepared for battle] against them. And the Federalist ranks were impressive. . . .

Among the stars and the patriot orators, it was Edmund Randolph who supplied the prime shock and surprise of the convention. The handsome young Governor was much beloved in his state. The great part he had played in Philadelphia was known to many; his refusal to sign the Constitution had become common knowledge; the *Virginia Gazette* in January, 1788, carried a letter with his reasons. But since then, Randolph had begun to waver; already he had been attacked in a newspaper for inconsistency. Yet no one knew for certain what the Governor's final decision would be. . . .

On June fourth, the first day of full debate, the Governor rose and made his declaration. It took him some time to reach his point. Plainly on the defensive, Randolph said he had not come hither [here] to apologize. . . . He was not a candidate for popularity. . . . If the Constitution were put before him as in Philadelphia—wholly to adopt or wholly to reject—he would again refuse his signature. But Massachusetts had urged amendments to be enacted by Congress *after* full ratification. For himself, he had originally been for *previous* amendments, to be approved by the several states before they ratified. But the postponement of this convention to so late a date made this impossible, "without inevitable ruin to the Union." Eight states had adopted the Constitution; they could not recede. He stood, then, to express his earnest endeavors for a firm, energetic government, and to concur in any practical scheme of amendments. Randolph, in short, was for the Constitution.

From this day on, no matter how it was argued, the base of difference between Federalists and Antifederalists in the Virginia convention would be "previous amendments" or "subsequent amendments"—whether the Constitution should be ratified as it stood, with amendments to be enacted later; or whether new state conventions should be called to alter the document before ratification.

From *Miracle at Philadelphia: The Story of the Constitutional Convention, May to September 1787* by Catherine Drinker Bowen. Copyright © 1966 by Catherine Drinker Bowen.

Critical Thinking

1. Why was Virginia's vote for ratification so important?
2. Why was Randolph's behavior a surprise to the other Virginians?
3. What was the argument between Federalists and Antifederalists regarding the question of amendments to the Constitution?

Connecting History and Literature

Answer one question with a brief essay.

A. How do you think the experience of the Revolution affected those who wrote the Constitution?
B. Why was compromise an important part of the process of writing and ratifying the Constitution?

WORKSHEET 12   **Primary Source**

Thomas Jefferson's First Inaugural Address

Thomas Jefferson was elected the third President of the United States in 1801. His Inaugural Address of March 4, 1801, set forth his views on government.

[The election] being now decided by the voice of the nation, announced according to the rules of the Constitution, all will . . . unite in common efforts for the common good. . . . [Al]though the will of the majority is in all cases to prevail, . . . the minority possess their equal rights, which equal law must protect, and to violate would be oppression. . . . If there be any among us who would wish to dissolve this Union or to change its republican form, let them stand undisturbed as monuments of the safety with which error of opinion may be tolerated where reason is left free to combat it. . . .

. . . It is proper you should understand what I deem the essential principles of our Government. . . . Equal and exact justice to all men of whatever state or persuasion, religious or political; peace, commerce and honest friendship with all nations, entangling alliances with none; . . . a jealous care of the right of election by the people . . . ; encouragement of agriculture, and of commerce . . . ; freedom of religion; freedom of the press, and freedom of person . . . , and trial by juries impartially selected. These principles form the bright constellation which has gone before us and guided our steps through an age of revolution and reformation.

From A Compilation of the Messages and Papers of the Presidents, 1789–1897, *edited by J. D. Richardson (U.S. Government Printing Office, Washington, D.C., 1896–1899), Vol. 1.*

Comprehension

1. What did Jefferson say about the rights of the minority?
2. What individual rights did Jefferson say should be upheld by the government?
3. What kind of relationship did Jefferson believe the United States should have with other nations?

Critical Thinking

4. In your own words, explain what Jefferson meant in saying, "let them [opponents of the Union or of republican government] stand undisturbed as monuments of the safety with which error of opinion may be tolerated where reason is left free to combat it."
5. Imagine that a Federalist, rather than Jefferson, had been elected President. In an Inaugural Address, what might this person have said about those who oppose the government?

WORKSHEET 12
Washington Irving, "Rip Van Winkle"

Literature

Washington Irving (1783-1859) was born in New York City and lived in this country until he was 32. He went to Europe in 1815 and stayed there for fifteen years. During this time he traveled to many countries, collecting fairy tales from each one he visited. The story of Rip Van Winkle is loosely based on the German folktale, "Peter Klaus." Irving set his story of Rip Van Winkle in the Revolutionary War period. He added descriptions of local customs and settings to create a uniquely American story of colonial life in the Catskill Mountains of New York. The story describes the strange experiences of a man who sleeps for twenty years and awakes to a world he no longer recognizes.

As he approached the village he met a number of people, but none whom he knew, which somewhat surprised him, for he had thought himself acquainted with every one in the country round. Their dress, too, was of a different fashion from that to which he was accustomed. They all stared at him with equal marks of surprise, and whenever they cast their eyes upon him, invariably stroked their chins. The constant recurrence of this gesture induced Rip, involuntarily, to do the same, when, to his astonishment, he found his beard had grown a foot long!

He had now entered the skirts of the village. A troop of strange children ran at his heels, hooting after him, and pointing at his gray beard. The dogs, too, not one of which he recognized for an old acquaintance, barked at him as he passed. The very village was altered; it was larger and more populous. There were rows of houses which he had never seen before, and those which had been his familiar haunts had disappeared. Strange names were over the doors— strange faces at the windows—every thing was strange. His mind now misgave him; he began to doubt whether both he and the world around him were not bewitched. Surely this was his native village, which he had left but the day before. There stood the Kaatskill mountains—there ran the silver Hudson at a distance—there was every hill and dale precisely as it had always been— Rip was sorely perplexed—"That flagon [jug] last night," thought he, "has addled my poor head sadly!"

It was with some difficulty that he found the way to his own house, which he approached with silent awe, expecting every moment to hear the shrill voice of Dame Van Winkle. He found the house gone to decay— the roof fallen in, the windows shattered, and the doors off the hinges. A half-starved dog that looked like Wolf was skulking about it. Rip called him by name, but the cur snarled, showed his teeth, and passed on. This was an unkind cut indeed—"My very dog," sighed poor Rip, "has forgotten me!"

He entered the house, which, to tell the truth, Dame Van Winkle had always kept in neat order. It was empty, forlorn, and apparently abandoned. This desolateness overcame all his connubial fears—he called loudly for his wife and children—the lonely chambers rang for a moment with his voice, and then all again was silence.

He now hurried forth, and hastened to his old resort, the village inn—but it too was gone. A large rickety wooden building stood in its place, with great gaping windows, some of them broken and mended with old hats and petticoats, and over the door was painted, "the Union Hotel, by Jonathan Doolittle." Instead of the great tree that used to shelter the quiet little Dutch inn of yore, there now was reared a tall naked pole, with something on the top that looked like a red night-cap, and from it was fluttering a flag, on which was a singular assemblage of stars and stripes—all this was strange and incomprehensible. He recognized on the sign, however, the ruby face of King George, under which he had smoked so many a peaceful pipe; but even this was singularly metamorphosed [changed]. The red coat was changed for one of blue and buff, a sword was held in the hand instead of a sceptre, the head was decorated with a cocked hat, and underneath was painted in large characters, GENERAL WASHINGTON.

There was, as usual, a crowd of folk about the door, but none that Rip recollected. The very character of the people seemed changed. There was a busy, bustling, disputatious tone about it, instead of the accustomed phlegm [lack of energy] and drowsy tranquillity. He looked in vain for the sage Nicholas Vedder, with his broad face, double chin and fair long pipe, uttering clouds of tobacco-smoke instead of idle speeches; or Van Bummel, the schoolmaster, doling forth the contents of an ancient newspaper. In place of these, a lean, bilious looking fellow, with his pockets full of handbills, was haranguing vehemently about rights of citizens—elections—members of congress—liberty—Bunker's Hill—heroes of seventy-six—and other words, which were a perfect Babylonish jargon to the bewildered Van Winkle.

The appearance of Rip, with his long grizzled beard, his rusty fowling-piece, his uncouth dress, and an army of women and children at his heels, soon attracted the attention of the tavern politicians. They crowded round him, eyeing him from head to foot with great curiosity. The orator bustled up to him, and, drawing him partly aside, inquired "on which side he voted?" Rip stared in vacant stupidity. Another short but busy little fellow pulled him by the arm, and, rising on tiptoe, inquired in his ear, "Whether he was Federal or Democrat?" Rip was equally at a loss to comprehend the question; when a knowing, self-important old gentleman, in a sharp cocked hat, made his way through the crowd, putting them to the right and left with his elbows as he passed, and planting himself before Van Winkle, with one arm akimbo, the other rest-

ing on his cane, his keen eyes and sharp hat penetrating, as it were, into his very soul, demanded in an austere tone, "what brought him to the election with a gun on his shoulder, and a mob at his heels, and whether he meant to breed a riot in the village?"—"Alas! gentlemen," cried Rip, somewhat dismayed, "I am a poor quiet man, a native of the place, and a loyal subject of the king, God bless him!"

Here a general shout burst from the bystanders—"A tory! a tory! a spy! a refugee! hustle him! away with him!" It was with great difficulty that the self-important man in the cocked hat restored order; and, having assumed a tenfold austerity of brow, demanded again of the unknown culprit, what he came there for, and whom he was seeking? The poor man humbly assured him that he meant no harm, but merely came there in search of some of his neighbors, who used to keep about the tavern.

"Well—who are they?—name them."

Rip bethought himself a moment, and inquired, "Where's Nicholas Vedder?"

There was a silence for a little while, when an old man replied, in a thin piping voice, "Nicholas Vedder! why, he is dead and gone these eighteen years! There was a wooden tombstone in the churchyard that used to tell all about him, but that's rotten and gone too."

"Where's Brom Dutcher?"

"Oh, he went off to the army in the beginning of the war; some say he was killed at the storming of Stony Point—others say he was drowned in a squall at the foot of Antony's Nose. I don't know—he never came back again."

"Where's Van Bummel, the schoolmaster?"

"He went off to the wars too, was a great militia general, and is now in congress."

Rip's heart died away at hearing of these sad changes in his home and friends, and finding himself thus alone in the world. Every answer puzzled him too, by treating of such enormous lapses of time, and of matters which he could not understand: war—congress—Stony Point;—he had no courage to ask after any more friends, but cried out in despair, "Does nobody here know Rip Van Winkle?"

"Oh, Rip Van Winkle!" exclaimed two or three, "Oh, to be sure! that's Rip Van Winkle yonder leaning against the tree."

Rip looked, and beheld a precise counterpart of himself, as he went up the mountain: apparently as lazy, and certainly as ragged. The poor fellow was now completely confounded. He doubted his own identity, and whether he was himself or another man. In the midst of his bewilderment, the man in the cocked hat demanded who he was, and what was his name?

"God knows," exclaimed he at his wit's end; "I'm not myself—I'm somebody else—that's me yonder—no—that's somebody else got into my shoes—I was myself last night, but I fell asleep on the mountain, and they've changed my gun, and every thing's changed, and I'm changed, and I can't tell what's my name, or who I am!"

The by-standers began now to look at each other, nod, wink significantly, and tap their fingers against their foreheads. There was a whisper, also, about securing the gun, and keeping the old fellow from doing mischief, at the very suggestion of which the self-important man in the cocked hat retired with some precipitation. At this critical moment a fresh comely woman passed through the throng to get a peep at the gray-bearded man. She had a chubby child in her arms, which, frightened at his looks, began to cry. "Hush, Rip," cried she, "hush, you little fool; the old man won't hurt you." The name of the child, the air of the mother, the tone of her voice, all awakened a train of recollections in his mind. "What is your name, my good woman?" asked he.

"Judith Gardenier."

"And your father's name?"

"Ah, poor man, Rip Van Winkle was his name, but it's twenty years since he went away from home with his gun, and never has been heard of since—his dog came home without him; but whether he shot himself, or was carried away by the Indians, nobody can tell. I was then but a little girl."

Rip had but one question more to ask; but he put it with a faltering voice:

"Where's your mother?"

"Oh, she too had died but a short time since; she broke a blood-vessel in a fit of passion at a New-England peddler."

There was a drop of comfort, at least, in this intelligence. The honest man could contain himself no longer. He caught his daughter and her child in his arms. "I am your father!" cried he—"Young Rip Van Winkle once old Rip Van Winkle now!—Does nobody know poor Rip Van Winkle?"

All stood amazed, until an old woman, tottering out from among the crowd, put her hand to her brow, and peering under it in his face for a moment, exclaimed, "Sure enough! it is Rip Van Winkle—it is himself! Welcome home again, old neighbor—Why, where have you been these twenty long years?"

Rip's story was soon told, for the whole twenty years had been to him but as one night. The neighbors stared when they heard it; some were seen to wink at each other, and put their tongues in their cheeks: and the self-important man in the cocked hat, who, when the alarm was over, had returned to the field, screwed down the corners of his mouth, and shook his head—upon which there was a general shaking of the head throughout the assemblage.

It was determined, however, to take the opinion of old Peter Vanderdonk, who was seen slowly advancing up the road. He was a descendant of the historian of that name, who wrote one of the earliest accounts of the province. Peter was the most ancient inhabitant of the village, and well versed in all the wonderful events and traditions of the neighborhood. He recollected Rip at once, and corroborated his story in the most satisfactory manner. He assured the company that it was a fact, handed down from his ancestor the historian, that the Kaatskill mountains had always been haunted by strange beings. That it was affirmed that the great Hendrick Hudson, the first discoverer of the river and country, kept a kind of vigil there every twenty years, with his crew of the Halfmoon; being permitted in this way to revisit the scenes of his enterprise, and keep a guardian eye upon the river, and the great city called by his name. That his father had once seen them in their old Dutch dresses playing at nine-pins in a hollow of the mountain; and that he himself had heard, one summer afternoon, the sound of their balls, like distant peals of thunder.

To make a long story short, the company broke up, and returned to the more important concerns of the election. Rip's daughter took him home to live with her; she had a snug, well-furnished house, and a stout cheery farmer for a husband, whom Rip recollected for one of the urchins that used to climb upon his back. As to Rip's son and heir, who was the ditto of himself, seen leaning against the tree, he was employed to work on the farm; but evinced [demonstrated] an hereditary disposition to attend to any thing else but his business.

Rip now resumed his old walks and habits; he soon found many of his former cronies, though all rather the worse for the wear and tear of time; and preferred making friends among the rising generation, with whom he soon grew into great favor.

Having nothing to do at home, and being arrived at that happy age when a man can be idle with impunity, he took his place once more on the bench at the inn door, and was reverenced as one of the patriarchs of the village, and a chronicle of the old times "before the war." It was some time before he could get into the regular track of gossip, or could be made to comprehend the strange events that had taken place during his torpor. How that there had been a revolutionary war—that the country had thrown off the yoke of old England—and that, instead of being a subject of His Majesty George the Third, he was now a free citizen of the United States.

Critical Thinking

1. What changes did Rip Van Winkle notice after he woke up? What things had not changed?
2. How did the townspeople react to Rip Van Winkle at first?
3. What national events had occurred while Rip Van Winkle slept?

Connecting History and Literature

Answer one question with a brief essay.

A. Imagine that Rip Van Winkle awoke in 1791. What "current events" information would he learn about?
B. If someone were to sleep for twenty years beginning today, what events might they miss?

WORSHEET 13
A Speech by Tecumseh

Shawnee Chief Tecumseh attempted to establish a confederation of eastern Indians against white encroachment of their lands. Tecumseh saw the British as allies in this endeavor and sided with them in the War of 1812. The following is an excerpt from a speech delivered by Tecumseh to his British allies in 1814.

Our Great Father, the King, is the head and you represent him. You always told us that you would never draw your foot off British ground; but now, Father, we see you are drawing back and we are sorry to see our Father doing so, without seeing the enemy. We must compare our Father's conduct to a fat animal that carries its tail upon its back; but when affrighted, it drops it between its legs and runs off.

Listen Father! The Americans have not yet defeated us by land; neither are we sure that they have done so by water; we therefore wish to remain here, and fight our enemy should they make their appearance. If they defeat us, we will then retreat with our Father. At the battle of the Rapids last war [1794] the Americans certainly defeat-

ed us; and when we retreated to our Father's fort at that place the gates were shut against us. We were afraid that it would now be the case; but instead of that we now see our British Father preparing to march out of his garrison.

Father! You have got the arms and ammunition which our Great Father sent for his red children. If you have an idea of going away, give them to us, and you may go and welcome for us. Our lives are in the hands of the Great Spirit. We are determined to defend our lands, and if it is his will, we wish to leave our bones upon them.

From Tecumseh's Last Stand, *by John Sugden (Norman: University of Oklahoma Press, 1985).*

Comprehension

1. Who was Tecumseh referring to when he used the names "Great Father" and "Father"?
2. What did Tecumseh say the British were preparing to do?
3. How did Tecumseh describe British conduct?
4. What actions did Tecumseh want the British to take?

Critical Thinking

5. Did Tecumseh consider the British reliable allies? Explain.
6. What was Tecumseh's goal?

WORKSHEET 13

Literature

Paul Horgan, *Great River*

Great River, by Paul Horgan, tells the history of the Rio Grande and the many peoples who have made that area their home. This selection deals with the many tasks of a woman on the American frontier.

When she wasn't cooking she was working toward cloth at her spinning wheel or loom; or making new garments; or mending old ones. It was said on the frontier that the first thing a young man did was to get him a wife so's to have her make him some clothes. When she wasn't sewing she was teaching the children their ABC's, and how to read, and how to cipher [add and subtract], and who the Lord Jesus was, and where their grandparents were, and what America was, and how a living was made. She had very little money and needed no more, for her husband obtained goods by trade; and what money they had was enough to pay the government, "as there were no unreasonable taxes." The mother told her young ones of what was dangerous in the surrounding country—wolves, snakes, big cats, bears. She made it plain that not all Indians were to be feared, for many went by on camping and hunting trips, and though queer and with outlandish notions, and a shock to see with all the cranky nakedness they showed, many of them were almost friends. She spoke of other kinds, of whom all had heard, who came with brand and scream and arrow and stolen rifle, to kill all who lived in a cabin like hers. Thinking of it, she raised her head, and put her hand under her children's chins and made them raise theirs, and said that fear was no excuse not to stay where you wanted to stay if you did no harm there, and bore your share of work. There were days when she even found time to surprise the children with a cornhusk doll, dressed and painted, or a rag doll that she had made for the girls; for the boys, perhaps a little horse made of twigs and a spool, or a toy bear stuffed with pine needles, or a beanbag, or a buckskin ball worked and worked until its seams met just right to create the sphere.

She kept her girls by her till late; her boys she lost early. The boys had hardly a cubhood. They went from boy to man; for as soon as their bodies were lengthening and filling to meet physical toil, they were ready to do a man's work; and were granted leave to do it. None could read the prickling thoughts of a youth or guess where they would turn him. The father watched his sons come to independence; and he saw this with pride, as an extension of the national ideal of equality and democratic opportunity. If the son wanted to stay at home to work, he was welcome; he was equally at liberty to do what many did at fourteen or fifteen—make a bundle of what he owned, take a rifle from the family's armory, and with a sweet bloom of ignorance on his confident face, go out on his own to a still farther West than the one he grew up in. He went with trading trains, or trapping parties, or with exploring expeditions of the Army, or joined a wild and dissolute crew of rivermen; and what he learned he measured by the gaunt, strong image of life to which he was born in the forest clearing, where in little he saw the community of work that in the large held America together. Everyone worked, and no job for man or woman was high or low, but all were respectable if honest. No one was embarrassed to work for pay. The President himself was paid.

From Great River, The Rio Grande in North American History *by Paul Horgan. Copyright © 1984 by Paul Horgan (Farrar Straus Giroux Inc.).*

Critical Thinking

1. Why did frontier women not need much money? What was money needed for?
2. What potential dangers were there on the frontier?
3. What kinds of work away from home might young men do?

Connecting History and Literature

Answer one question with a brief essay.

A. What personal qualities did both explorers and frontier settlers need to survive?

B. Explain what Horgan meant by "the community of work that . . . held America together."

Name _____   Date _____

WORKSHEET 14

Life and Work in New England Mills

An observer visited mills in Lowell, Massachusetts, and Manchester, New Hampshire, in 1836. The following is taken from his account, which appeared in the magazine *The Harbinger.*

In Lowell live between seven and eight thousand young women, who are generally daughters of farmers of the different states of New England. . . .

The operatives work thirteen hours a day in the summer time, and from daylight to dark in the winter. At halfpast four in the morning the factory bell rings, and at five the girls must be in the mills. A clerk, placed as a watch, observes those who are a few minutes behind the time, and effectual means are taken to stimulate to punctuality. This is the morning commencement of the industrial discipline (should we not rather say industrial tyranny?) which is established. . . . At seven the girls are allowed thirty minutes for breakfast, and at noon thirty minutes more for dinner, except during the first quarter of the year, when the time is extended to forty-five minutes. But within this time they must hurry to their boardinghouses and return to the factory, and that through the hot sun or the rain or the cold. A meal eaten under such circumstances must be quite unfavorable to digestion and health. . . . At seven o'clock in the evening the factory bell sounds the close of the day's work.

Thus thirteen hours per day of close attention and monotonous labor are exacted from the young women in these manufactories. . . . So fatigued . . . are numbers of girls that they go to bed soon after their evening meal, and endeavor by a comparatively long sleep to resuscitate their weakened frames for the toil of the coming day. . . .

Now let us examine the nature of the labor itself, and the conditions under which it is performed. . . . The largest that we saw is in the Amoskeag Mills at Manchester. . . . The din and clatter of these five hundred looms, under full operation, struck us on first entering as something frightful and infernal. . . . After a while we became somewhat inured to it, and by speaking quite close to the ear of an operative and quite loud, we could hold a conversation and make the inquiries we wished.

The girls attend upon an average three looms; many attend four, but this requires a very active person, and the most unremitting care. However, a great many do it. Attention to two is as much as should be demanded of an operative. This gives us some idea of the application required during the thirteen hours of daily labor. The atmosphere of such a room cannot of course be pure; . . . it is charged with cotton filaments and dust, which, we are told, are very injurious to the lungs.

From The Harbinger, *November 14, 1836.*

Comprehension

1. At what time does work start in the mills? When does it end?
2. How much time do the workers have for themselves? What do they do then?
3. What health problems does the writer describe in the factory?

Critical Thinking

4. What is the writer's opinion of the mill system? Give examples from the passage to support your answer.
5. If you worked in the Amoskeag Mills, what might you do to make your life more bearable?

WORKSHEET 14
Margaret Walker, *Jubilee*

Literature

Jubilee, a novel by Margaret Walker, was written in 1966. It tells the story of the author's own ancestors, including Vyry, a slave on a Georgia plantation belonging to "Marse John" and his wife, "Big Missy."

Early in the spring of 1851 a fairly well-developed plot for an uprising among the slaves of Lee County, with the assistance of free Negroes and white abolitionists, became known to the High Sheriff of the county. How the news began to leak out and through what sources could not be determined by most Negroes. In the first place, the slaves on Marse John's plantation were not fully informed as to what nature the plot took nor how an uprising could take place. Brother Zeke was so troubled that he confided to his flock at their regular meeting place at the Rising Glory Church that it must be a false rumor since no definite plans had ever come to his knowledge. It was first suspected, however, by the guards . . . and the drivers, who claimed that the Negroes were unusually hard to manage. And the neighboring whites claimed there were unusual movements in town among strange whites and in the county among free Negroes. At first the planters were not suspicious and hardly dared believe the piece-meal information they received. Why would their slaves want to do such a thing?

As Big Missy said to Marse John, "They are all well treated, and we love them and take good care of them just like a part of our family. When they are sick we nurse them back to health. We feed and clothe them and teach them the Christian religion. Our nigras are good and wouldn't try such a thing unless some criminal minds aided and abetted [encouraged] them." . . . Such monstrous activities were beyond the wildest imaginations of their good and happy child-like slaves!

Nevertheless, if there was such ingratitude lurking among them, after all the money that had been spent on food and clothes and doctor bills, the owners must be realistic and resort to drastic methods to counteract such activity. They must not wait too long to listen to reason. Hastily and secretly, Marse John and his planter friends gathered with this purpose. There they decided, as their drivers had suggested, that the first thing was to seek out the culprits and see that they were punished to the full extent of the law, chiefly by hanging. Thus they would make an example of them and put the fear of God in the rest of the slaves. Second, they must clamp down harder on the movements of all blacks, enforce the curfew laws and all of the Black Code, thereby rigorously maintaining control over their property, both land and chattel [property] slaves. Finally, but not least, they must seek out all abolitionists guilty of giving aid and comfort to the black enemies of the Georgia people, and either force them out of the state or deal with them so harshly that they would willingly leave. . . .

The darkest day in Vyry's young life came without warning. Big Missy and Marse John had arranged to sell Aunt Sally. She would go first to Savannah and then by boat to New Orleans, where she would go on the auction block and be sold to the highest bidder. The morning she was ordered to go, she and Vyry went as usual to the kitchen. Big Missy came out in the kitchen after breakfast and told Aunt Sally to get her things together; there was a wagon in the backyard waiting to take her to Savannah. Now Aunt Sally was ready. She had her head-rag on and she had tied in a bundle the few things she had in the world including the few rags of clothes she wore. She had spread out one of her big aprons and tied them in it. Now she carried it in her arms. Tears were running down her fat black cheeks and she could not control her trembling lips. Vyry stood dazed and numb. Even when Aunt Sally hugged and kissed her, Vyry did not cry. She could not believe this was real, that she would be forced apart from Aunt Sally, that Aunt Sally was leaving and going somewhere. She heard Aunt Sally saying, "Goodbye, honey, don't yall forget to pray. Pray to God to send his chilluns a Moses; pray to Jesus to have mercy on us poor suffering chilluns. Goodbye, honey, don't you forget Aunt Sally and don't forget to pray. Aunt Sally know she ain't never gwine see yall no more in this here sinful world, but I'm gwine be waiting for you on the other side where there ain't gwine be no more auction block. Goodbye, honey-child, goodbye."

Even then Vyry's eyes were dry. But then she saw poor old Aunt Sally clinging to Sam and Big Boy. She heard her sobbing pitifully, "Oh Lord, when is you gwine send us that Moses? When you gwine set us peoples free? Jesus, how long? Marster, how long? They is taking all I got in the world from me, they is sending me way down yonder to that cruel auction block! Oh, Lord, how long is we gotta pray?" They were pulling her away but stumbling along crying and muttering she kept saying, "Oh, Lord, have mercy!"

Then Vyry found herself shaking like a leaf in a whirlwind. Salt tears were running in her mouth, and her short, sharp finger nails were digging in the palms of her hands. Suddenly she decided she would go with Aunt Sally, and just then Big Missy slapped her so hard she saw stars and when she saw straight again Aunt Sally was gone.

From Jubilee *by Margaret Walker. Copyright ©1966 by Margaret Walker Alexander. Published by Houghton Mifflin Company.*

Critical Thinking

1. Why did Big Missy say her slaves would never want to rebel? Do you think she was right? Why or why not?
2. How did the slaveowners respond to rumors of an uprising?
3. How did Vyry react when Aunt was sold away? How did Aunt Sally react? Why, in your opinion, would slaveowners break up friendships and families in this way?

Connecting History and Literature

Answer one question with a brief essay.

A. Why did slavery become more important in the South during the early 1800s?
B. What was Nat Turner's Rebellion? What were its effects?

WORKSHEET 15   **Primary Source**
Daniel Webster Defends the Union

John C. Calhoun advocated a strong national government early in his career and later switched to the doctrine of states' rights. Daniel Webster moved in the opposite direction: from support of states' rights to support of a strong Union. The following selection is excerpted from Webster's second reply to Senator Robert Hayne of South Carolina, made on January 26, 1830.

This leads us to inquire into the origin of this government and the source of its power. Whose agent is it? Is it the creature of the State Legislatures, or the creature of the people? If the Government of the United States be the agent of the State governments, then they may control it, provided they can agree in the manner of controlling it; if it be the agent of the people, then the people alone can control it, restrain it, modify it, or reform it. It is observable enough, that the doctrine for which the honorable gentleman contends leads him to the necessity of maintaining, not only that this General Government is the creature of the States, but that it is the creature of each of the States, severally, so that each may assert the power for itself of determining whether it acts within the limits of its authority. It is the servant of four-and-twenty masters, of different wills and different purposes, and yet bound to obey all. This absurdity . . . arises from a misconception as to the origin of this government and its true character. It is, sir, the people's Constitution, the people's government, made for the people, made by the people, and answerable to the people. . . .

I have not allowed myself, sir, to look beyond the Union, to see what might lie hid-

den in the dark recess behind. . . . While the Union lasts, we have high, exciting, gratifying prospects spread out before us, for us and our children. Beyond that, I seek not to penetrate the veil. . . . When my eyes shall be turned to behold for the last times the sun in heaven, may I not see him shining on the broken and dishonored fragments of a once glorious Union; on states dissevered, discordant, belligerent; on a land rent with civil feuds, or drenched, it may be, in fraternal blood! Let their last feeble and lingering glance rather behold the gorgeous ensign of the republic, now known and honored throughout the earth, still full high advanced, its arms and trophies streaming in their original luster, not a stripe erased or polluted, nor a single star obscured, bearing for its motto no such miserable interrogatory as, What is all this worth? nor those other words of delusion and folly, Liberty first, and Union afterward; but everywhere, spread all over in characters of living light, blazing on all its ample folds, as they float over the sea and over the land . . . that other sentiment, dear to every true American heart—Liberty *and* Union, now and forever, one and inseparable!

Reprinted in Living Ideas in America, *edited by Henry Steele Commager (New York: Harper & Row, 1964).*

Comprehension

1. What arguments against the idea of states' rights did Webster put forth?
2. Why did Webster oppose the motto *Liberty first, and Union afterward*?
3. What words in Webster's speech foreshadow the Civil War?

Critical Thinking

4. What issues of national policy cause debate in our country today? Are these issues based in sectional differences?

WORSHEET 15

Literature

Elizabeth Sullivan, A Story of the Trail of Tears

Elizabeth Sullivan, a Creek Indian, collected the stories told to her by her great-grandmother and other older Creeks in the book *Indian Legends of the Trail of Tears and Other Creek Stories*. The following passage is the story of a seven-year-old girl's experiences on the Trail of Tears.

When the removal began Annakee could not understand all the changes taking place. She only knew her grandmother's eyes were bloodshot, her cheeks sunken, her lips cracked. Annakee held closely to her grandmother's hand as they walked on with so many Indians. Some she did not know. Everyone appeared fearful and sad. She saw many crying. Annakee began to suffer from irritating mosquito bites. She would scratch mercilessly until she bled. Her little legs were so tired and her feet ached.

At night she saw the stars in the sky that used to twinkle and shine like dew drops in the rainbow as her grandmother's tales had told about the mystery of the heavenly bodies. But tonight the stars appeared dim and seemed to be hiding from her as she looked up in the sky.

Annakee remembered her home. The corn crib was full of corn. They had plenty of dried fruit and meat. Her father and mother saw to that. Her two older brothers were hunting all of the time. They even knew how to shoot with bow and arrow to kill fish when they came up for air after shoe string roots had been pounded and put into the river up stream and a dam was made. . . .

"God lives, Creator of all things, be fearful and pray." They sang songs in whispers not audible to the soldiers who would camp nearby. The aroma of the soldiers' food reached them and hunger became almost unbearable.

Her grandmother was very stern and told her—"Learn never to cry, even if you are hurt or hungry. Never look back to see what is going on in the back." This she learned very quickly. . . .

In the dense forest Annakee saw strange birds, different-shaped leaves than she had ever seen. She asked her grandmother about it. Her grandmother held her very close by the campfire and told her that they had come far far away from home and they would never see their homeland and advised her to be brave and never cry.

"Legend of the Trail of Tears" from Indian Legends of the Trail of Tears and Other Stories as told by Elizabeth Sullivan. Copyright © 1974 by Elizabeth Sullivan. Published in The Third Woman: Minority Women Writers of The United States, *edited by Dexter Fisher. Copyright © 1980 by Houghton Mifflin Company.*

Critical Thinking

1. How did Annakee figure out that something was wrong?
2. What were the hardships of the Trail of Tears?
3. Why did Annakee's grandmother tell Annakee never to cry?
4. What did Annakee remember about her home? Why did she have that particular memory?

Connecting History and Literature

Answer one question with a brief essay.

A. Why did the government relocate the Indians?
B. How did different Indian peoples react to the relocation order?

Name _____   Date _____

WORKSHEET 16   **Primary Source**
Dorothea Dix Pleads for Humane Treatment of the Insane

Dorothea Dix spent eighteen months traveling throughout Massachusetts, investigating conditions of the insane. The following selection is
excerpted from the report that Dix wrote to the Massachusetts legislature
in 1843. Since it was considered unladylike for women to address the legislature, friends of Miss Dix delivered the report for her.

I come to present the strong claims of suffering humanity. I come to place before the legislature of Massachusetts the condition of
the miserable, the desolate, the outcast. I
come as the advocate of helpless, forgotten,
insane, and idiotic men and women; of
beings sunk to a condition from which the
most unconcerned would start with real
horror; of beings wretched in our prisons,
and more wretched in our almshouses [poor-
houses]. . . .

I proceed, gentlemen, briefly to call your
attention to the *present* state of insane persons confined within this Commonwealth,
in *cages, closets, cellars, stalls, pens!
Chained,* naked, beaten with rods, *and*
lashed into obedience. . . .

It is the Commonwealth, not its integral
parts, that is accountable for most of the
abuses which have lately and still do exist. I
repeat it, it is defective legislation which
perpetuates and multiplies these abuses. In
illustration of my subject, I offer the following extracts from my Notebook and Journal:

. . . *Lincoln.* A woman in a cage. *Medford.*
One idiotic subject chained, and one in a
closed stall for seventeen years. *Pepperell.*
One often doubly chained, hand and foot;
another violent; several peaceable now.

Brookfield. One man chained, comfortable.
Granville. One often closely confined; now
losing the use of his limbs from want of exer-
cise. *Charlemont.* One man caged. *Savoy.*
One man caged. *Lenox.* Two in the jail,
against whose unfit condition there the jail-
er protests. . . .

Newburyport. Visited the almshouse. . . .
The . . . subject was a woman in a cellar. . . .
In that contracted space, unlighted, unven-
tilated, she poured forth the wailings of
despair. Mournfully she extended her arms
and appealed to me. "Why am I consigned to
hell? . . . "

It is not few, but many, it is not a part, but
the whole, who bear unqualified testimony
to this evil. A voice strong and deep comes
up from every almshouse and prison in
Massachusetts where the insane are or have
been protesting against such evils as have
been illustrated in the preceding pages.

Gentlemen, I commit you to this sacred
cause. Your action upon this subject will
affect the present and future condition of
hundreds and of thousands.

*From "Plea for Human Treatment of the Insane" by
Dorothea Dix, in* Annals of America, *Vol. 7(Chicago:
Encyclopedia Britannica, 1968).*

Comprehension

1. What were some of the conditions to
   which Dix objected?
2. Why, according to Dix, was the Massachusetts legislature responsible for
   these abuses?

Critical Thinking

3. If Dix had found insane persons housed
   in a jail, yet properly treated, would
   she still have objected? Explain.
4. Why are disadvantaged groups especially vulnerable to mistreatment?

WORSHEET 16

Literature

William Jay Jacobs, The Fight for Women's Suffrage

William Jay Jacobs' book *Mother, Aunt Susan, and Me* tells the story of
Elizabeth Cady Stanton and Susan B. Anthony and their organization of
the women's suffrage movement. This move led eventually to the Nine-
teenth Amendment (1920), which gave women the right to vote. As part of
the struggle for this right, Anthony broke the law by voting in the 1872
presidential election and was arrested. This excerpt from *Mother, Aunt
Susan, and Me* tells the story of Susan's trial.

Justice Ward Hunt presided as trial judge.
Henry B. Selden served as Susan B. Anthony's chief attorney. Mr. Selden said that
when Susan voted she thought she had a
right to vote. So what she *did* could not be
considered a crime. She was putting her idea
to a test. Susan B. Anthony was no criminal.
Moreover, women legally *did* have the right
to vote, he said, according to the Constitution.

Mr. Selden's speech was clear, logical, and
to the point. For more than three hours he
spoke eloquently.

But Judge Hunt hardly listened at all.
Instead, he read a statement that he had
prepared before coming into court—before
he had heard the argument for the defense.

Then he ordered the all-male jury to find
Susan B. Anthony guilty as charged.

Mr. Selden jumped to his feet. "I object! I
object!" he shouted. "No judge has a right in
a criminal case to tell a jury what to decide.
I demand that the members of the jury be
allowed to vote."

But Judge Hunt dismissed the jury without letting one of its members speak.

The next day Susan's lawyers asked for a
new trial. Judge Hunt turned down the
request. He then ordered Susan to stand for
sentencing. "Has the prisoner anything to
say why sentence shall not be pronounced?"
asked Judge Hunt.

Susan, dressed in black except for a trim-
ming of white lace at her neckline, paused
for an instant. Then she spoke firmly and
forcefully.

"Yes, Your Honor, I have many things to
say: for in your ordered verdict of guilty you

have trampled under foot every vital princi-
ple of our government. My natural rights,
my civil rights, my political rights, my judi-
cial rights are all alike ignored."

Judge Hunt, impatient, interrupted.
Pointing at the accused, he declared, "The
Court cannot allow the prisoner to go on."

But Susan would not stop. Since the day
of her arrest she had been given no chance
to defend herself. Judge Hunt had not even
allowed her to be a witness for herself at the
trial.

"The prisoner must sit down—the Court
cannot allow it," bellowed Judge Hunt.

Susan continued: "Had Your Honor sub-
mitted my case to the jury, as was clearly
your duty, even then I should have had just
cause of protest, for not one of those men was
my peer; but native or foreign born, white or
black, rich or poor, educated or ignorant,
sober or drunk, each and every man of them
was my political superior. . . . Under such
circumstances a commoner in England, tried
before a jury of lords, would have far less
cause to complain than have I, a woman,
tried before a jury of men."

"The Court must insist," Judge Hunt
interrupted again. "The prisoner has been
tried according to the established forms of
the law."

"Yes, Your Honor," answered Susan, "but
by forms of law all made by men, interpret-
ed by men, in favor of men, and against
women."

"The Court orders the prisoner to sit
down. It will not allow another word!" shouted Judge Hunt, banging his gavel for order.

Susan had a final word. She had expected, she said, a fair trial and justice. "But failing to get this justice . . . I ask not leniency at your hands but rather the full rigor of the law."

"The Court must insist . . . " started Judge Hunt. At that point Susan sat down.

"The prisoner will stand up," directed the judge.

Again she rose.

"The sentence of the Court is that you pay a fine of one hundred dollars and the costs of prosecution."

"May it please Your Honor," began Susan. "I will never pay a dollar of your unjust penalty. All l possess is a debt of ten thousand dollars incurred by publishing my paper—*The Revolution*—the sole object of which was to educate all women to do precisely as I have done, rebel against your man-made, unjust, unconstitutional forms of law, which tax, fine, imprison, and hang women, while denying them the right of representation in the government."

Susan, remaining calm, but with her voice rising in defiance, then concluded: "I will work on with might and main to pay every dollar of that honest debt, but not a penny shall go to this unjust claim. And I shall earnestly and persistently continue to urge all women to the practical recognition of the old Revolutionary maxim, 'Resistance to tyranny is obedience to God.' "

For a moment the courtroom was hushed in silence. Later we heard that even some members of the jury said they had felt like applauding, perhaps even cheering out loud.

From Mother, Aunt Susan, and Me: The First Fight for Women's Rights. *Copyright © 1979 by William Jay Jacobs. Reprinted by permission of Coward-McCann, Inc.*

Critical Thinking

1. Why did Susan B. Anthony's trial take so little time?
2. Why, according to Anthony, would the trial have been unfair even if the jury had been allowed to decide the case?
3. Why, in your opinion, did Anthony demand that she be punished with "the full rigor of the law"?

Connecting History and Literature

Answer one question with a brief essay.

A. What were the links between the abolitionist movement and the movement for women's rights?
B. Why, in your opinion, did it take so long for women to gain the right to vote?

WORSHEET 17
A Soldier's Letters During the Mexican War

Primary Source

The excerpts below, from the letters of 25-year-old Barna Upton of Charlemont, Massachusetts, make up one of the few eyewitness accounts of the Mexican War from the point of view of the average soldier. Upton enlisted in the army in 1845 because he wanted to see the world and pursue adventure. At the time of his enlistment, he had never been outside of New England. Upton was mortally wounded in the final charge on Mexico City in September 1847.

Matamoros
July 29,1846

[Dear Father:] . . . I am perfectly satisfied with my situation. It suits my taste for saving and adventure. Besides, I am in the finest country in the world—a healthy climate (a little too warm though, sometimes) and surrounded by the varied productions of a southern clime. I march over almost boundless prairies, across large rivers without scarce knowing their names. I see countless herds of buffalo, deer, and wild horses moving unmolested over the mighty plains. . . .

Camargo, Mexico
August 28,1846

Dear Friends: I am well. Our brigade is about to move for Monterrey. I shall not have another opportunity [to write] for a long time. We arrived at this place after a hard march of nine days. The distance is about one hundred twenty miles. A part of the Army has already moved on its way to the interior. . . .

There is a good many sick in the Army,

though there is no dangerous disease and but few deaths in proportion to the great number of men. I believe the enemy are determined to make every exertion to prevent our Army from advancing into their country. We shall no doubt have some hard fighting. All the troops here seem anxious to be led on to the fray. Is it not sad to think how many, either in battle or by disease, will lay their eye in the sand (as the soldiers say) before the close of this extensive campaign? I realize that my own chance is with the rest in the lottery of life and death, yet let what will happen, I shall always be found doing my duty.

I think it is the duty now for the Mexicans to prevent if they can an invasion of their country, yet in the first place it was their own haughtiness, stubbornness, . . . and foolish, ignorant pride that was the immediate cause of hostilities. They acted like a little snappish puppy biting at a man's heels. . . .

From "Our First Foreign War" edited by William F. Goetzmann in American Heritage, June 1966, Vol. XVII. (American Heritage Publishing Company, Inc.).

Comprehension

1. What were some of the things that Upton saw while in the army, as described in the letter to his father?
2. What hardships of army life did Upton mention?
3. According to Upton, how did the American army feel about fighting?
4. What were Upton's opinions about the Mexicans?

Critical Thinking

5. Do you think Upton believed that he had satisfied his desire for adventure? Explain your answer.
6. How did Upton feel about death?
7. If you had to write an epitaph for Barna Upton's gravestone, what would it say?

WORKSHEET 17   **Literature**
Richard Henry Dana, Jr., *Two Years Before the Mast*

During the nation's westward expansion, American writers produced a literature of the frontier. Aristocratic New Englander Richard Henry Dana, Jr., wrote *Two Years Before the Mast,* a classic account of American seafaring in the early 1800s. In this excerpt, Dana describes his ship's stop in Monterey, California.

It was a fine Saturday afternoon that we came to anchor, the sun about an hour high, and everything looking pleasantly. The Mexican flag was flying from the little square presidio [fortress], and the drums and trumpets of the soldiers, who were out on parade, sounded over the water, and gave great life to the scene. Everyone was delighted with the appearance of things. We felt as though we had got into a Christian (which in the sailor's vocabulary means civilized) country. . . .

The next day . . . we began trading. . . . For a week or ten days all was life on board. The people came off to look and to buy. . . . Our cargo was an assorted one; that is, it consisted of everything under the sun. We had spirits of all kinds (sold by the cask [barrel]), teas, coffee, sugars, spices, raisins, molasses, hardware, crockeryware, tin-ware, cutlery . . . shawls, scarfs, necklaces, jewelry, and combs for the women; furniture; and, in fact, everything that can be imagined, from Chinese fireworks to English cartwheels—of which we had a dozen pairs with their iron tires on.

The Californians are an idle, thriftless people, and can make nothing for themselves. The country abounds in grapes, yet they buy, at a great price, bad wine made in Boston and brought round by us. . . . Their hides, too, which they value at two dollars in money, they barter for something which costs seventy-five cents in Boston; and buy shoes (as like as not made of their own hides, which have been carried twice round Cape Horn) at three and four dollars. . . .

Every town has a presidio in its centre; or rather every presidio has a town built around it; for the forts were first built by the Mexican government, and then the people built near them, for protection. The presidio here was entirely open and unfortified. . . . Each town has a commandant . . . while two or three alcaldes and corregidores, elected by the inhabitants, are the civil officers. . . . No Protestant has any political rights, nor can he hold property, or, indeed, remain more than a few weeks on shore, unless he belong to a foreign vessel. Consequently, Americans and English who intend to reside here, become Papists [Catholics]—the current phrase among them being, "A man must leave his conscience at Cape Horn."

But, to return to Monterey. The houses here, as everywhere else in California, are of one story, built of *adobes*. . . . The Indians . . . do all the hard work, two or three being attached to the better house[s]; and the poorest persons are able to keep one, at least, for they have only to feed them, and give them a small piece of coarse cloth. . . .

In Monterey there are a number of English and Americans . . . who have married Californians, become united to the Roman Church, and acquired considerable property. Having more industry, frugality [thriftiness], and enterprise than the natives, they soon get nearly all the trade into their hands. They usually keep shops, in which they retail the goods purchased in the larger quantities from our vessels, and also send a good deal into the interior, taking hides in pay, which they again barter with our ships. In every town on the coast there are foreigners engaged in this kind of trade, while I recollect but two shops kept by natives. The people are naturally suspicious of foreigners, and they would not be allowed to remain, were it not that they conform to the Church, and by marrying natives, and bringing up their children as Roman Catholics and Mexicans, and not teaching them the English language, that they quiet suspicion, and even become popular and leading men.

The chief alcaldes in Monterey and Santa Barbara were Yankees by birth.

From Two Years Before the Mast, A Personal Narrative of Life at Sea *by Richard Henry Dana, Jr. (Harper, 1840).*

Critical Thinking

1. What prejudices are there in Dana's observations of the people of California?
2. What prejudices and class distinctions existed among the Californians?
3. Do you think Dana supported United States expansion westward? Explain.

Connecting History and Literature

Answer one question with a brief essay.

A. How had Mexican independence affected trade in areas such as California?
B. What events in Texas and other parts of the West during the 1830s and early 1840s signaled rising U.S. interest in these areas?

WORSHEET 18
Constitution of the Confederate States of America

The founders of the Confederate States of America wrote a constitution similar to the U.S. Constitution. The differences indicate how the South wanted to change the structure of government.

Preamble

We, the people of the Confederate States, each State acting in its sovereign and independent character, in order to form a permanent federal government, establish justice, insure domestic tranquillity, and secure the blessings of liberty to ourselves and our posterity—invoking the favor and guidance of Almighty God—do ordain and establish this Constitution for the Confederate States of America. . . .

Article l, Section 8, Clauses 1 and 3
—The Congress shall have power—
(1) To lay and collect taxes, duties, imposts, and excises, for revenue necessary to pay the debts, provide for the common defence, and carry on the Government of the Confederate States; but no bounties shall be granted from the treasury; nor shall any duties or taxes on importations from foreign nations be laid to promote or foster any branch of industry; and all duties, imposts, and excises shall be uniform throughout the Confederate States. . . .
(3) To regulate commerce with foreign nations, and among the several States, and with the Indian tribes; but neither this, nor any other clause contained in the Constitu-

tion shall be construed to delegate the power to Congress to appropriate money for any internal improvement intended to facilitate commerce. . . .

Article IV, Section 3, Clause 3
(3) The Confederate States may acquire new territory; and Congress shall have power to legislate and provide governments for the inhabitants of all territory belonging to the Confederate States, lying within the limits of the several States, and may permit them, at such times, and in such manner as it may by law provide, to form States to be admitted into the Confederacy. In all such territory, the institution of negro slavery, as it now exists in the Confederate States, shall be recognized and protected by Congress and by the territorial government; and the inhabitants of the several Confederate States and Territories shall have the right to take to such territory any slaves lawfully held by them in any of the States or Territories of the Confederate States.

Quoted in Documents of American History to 1898, *Vol. I, edited by Henry Steele Commager and Milton Cantor (Prentice-Hall, 1988).*

Comprehension

1. What phrase in the preamble emphasizes the issue of states' rights?
2. Which article, section, and clause focuses on the collection of tariffs?
3. Which article, section, and clause deals with the extension of slavery?

Critical Thinking

4. From your knowledge of the South's feelings about tariffs, explain how the clause about tariffs would satisfy the South.

WORKSHEET 18   **Literature**
Harriet Jacobs, *Incidents in the Life of a Slave Girl*

Fiery speeches, impassioned essays, and moving books such as *Uncle Tom's Cabin* helped build antislavery sentiment before the Civil War. Abolitionist literature also included narratives by former slaves. With help from editor Lydia Maria Child, Harriet Jacobs published *Incidents in the Life of a Slave Girl* in 1861, disguising the names of people and places, and using the pseudonym of Linda Brent. It describes her life in the South, her seven years spent in hiding from her master, and her escape to the North and eventual freedom. The following scene describes her life in New York after passage of the Fugitive Slave Law.

On my return from Rochester [to New York City], I called at the house of Mr. Bruce. . . . Mr. Bruce had married again, and it was proposed that I should become nurse to a new infant. I had but one hesitation, and that was my feeling of insecurity in New York, now greatly increased by the passage of the Fugitive Slave Law. However, I resolved to try the experiment. I was again fortunate in my employer. The new Mrs. Bruce was an American, brought up under aristocratic influences, . . . but if she had any prejudice against color, I was never made aware of it; and as for the system of slavery, she had a most hearty dislike of it. . . .

About the time that I reentered the Bruce family, an event occurred of disastrous import to the colored people. The slave Hamlin, the first fugitive that came under the new law, was given up by the bloodhounds [slavecatchers] of the North to the bloodhounds of the South. It was the beginning of a reign of terror to the colored population.

Many a poor washerwoman who, by hard labor, had made herself a comfortable home, was obliged to sacrifice her furniture, bid a hurried farewell to friends, and seek her fortune among strangers in Canada. Many a wife discovered a secret she had never known before—that her husband was a fugitive, and must leave her to insure his own safety. Worse still, many a husband discovered that his wife had fled from slavery years ago, and as "the child follows the condition of its mother," the children of his love

were liable to be seized and carried into slavery.

All that winter I lived in a state of anxiety. When I took the children out to breathe the air, I closely observed the countenances [faces] of all I met. I dreaded the approach of summer, when snakes and slaveholders make their appearance. I was, in fact, a slave in New York, as subject to slave laws as I had been in a Slave State. Strange incongruity in a State called free!

Spring returned, and I received warning from the South that Dr. Flint [her owner] knew of my return to my old place, and was making preparations to have me caught. . . .

I immediately informed Mrs. Bruce of my danger, and she took prompt measures for my safety. . . .

I was sent into New England, where I was sheltered by the wife of a senator, whom I shall always hold in grateful remembrance. . . .

Some months after I returned from my flight to New England, I received a letter from [my grandmother], in which she wrote, "Dr. Flint is dead. He has left a distressed family. Poor old man! I hope he made his peace with God.". . .

I thought to myself that she was a better Christian than I was, if she could entirely forgive him. . . . There are wrongs which even the grave does not bury. . . .

His departure from this world did not diminish my danger. He had threatened my grandmother that his heirs should hold me in slavery after he was gone; that I never should be free so long as a child of his survived. . . .

I kept close watch of the newspapers for arrivals. . . . Reader, if you have never been a slave, you cannot imagine the acute sensation of suffering at my heart, when I read the names of Mr. and Mrs. Dodge [Flint's daughter], at a hotel in Courtland Street. It was a third-rate hotel, and that circumstance convinced me of the truth of what I had heard, that they were short of funds and had need of my value, as *they* valued me; and

that was by dollars and cents. . . . It was impossible to tell how near the enemy was. He might have passed and repassed the house while we were sleeping. He might at that moment be waiting to pounce upon me if I ventured out of doors.

From Incidents in the Life of a Slave Girl (Written by Herself) *by Harriet Jacobs (Linda Brent), edited by L. Maria Child (1561). Reproduced from the original, with an introduction by Valerie Smith (Oxford University Press, 1955).*

Critical Thinking

1. Why did the arrest of the slave Hamlin alarm Jacobs?
2. According to this account, what kind of treatment could southern slaves expect from northerners?
3. What explanation do you suppose the members of the Flint family would have given for their efforts to recapture Harriet Jacobs?

Connecting History and Literature

Answer one question with a brief essay.

A. Why would Jacobs have changed the names of real people and places when her book was published in 1861?
B. What effect did the Fugitive Slave Law have even on slaves who had escaped safely to free states in the North?

WORKSHEET 19
Remembering Abraham Lincoln

Every morning Lincoln crossed the street from the White House to the War Department telegraph office to read the dispatches of the previous night. Albert Chandler, a telegrapher in that office, wrote an account of his memories of President Lincoln, parts of which are reprinted below.

[Mr. Lincoln's] keen sense of the ridiculous extended to little things, and he was as perfect a mimic as his large frame would permit. A good example was this: Albert Johnson, Mr. Stanton's private secretary . . . , was a man of unusually small stature, weighing perhaps a hundred and ten pounds, and his deportment was extremely polite. On one occasion Mr. Lincoln wanted to refer to the Bible, and he asked Johnson to bring it. Johnson danced out of the room to get it; but not finding it quickly, and fearing that the President might become impatient, he ran back to explain that he had not found it yet, but would have it presently. He finally brought it, with an apology for the delay, and, with low repeated bows, retired. After Mr. Lincoln had made the desired use of the book, he ran nimbly into the adjoining room, just as Johnson had done, reappeared, then made his delivery of the book in the same fashion, greatly to his own and our amusement. This may not strike anybody as funny; but the extreme contrast in the size and movements of the two men, and the close imitation of the mimicry, made it decidedly appear so to us. . . .

On June 14, 1863, information of the extensive movement of the Confederate army toward Maryland and Pennsylvania was received. This . . . culminated in the great Battle of Gettysburg. From the beginning of this movement until the recrossing of the Potomac by General Lee, with all that remained of his army, Mr. Lincoln spent much of his life in the War Department telegraph office. . . .

On July 12, upon receiving a message from General Meade explaining somewhat in detail the movements of his army, and of the enemy as far as he could ascertain them, [Mr. Lincoln] called me to a large map hanging near my desk . . . and pointed out that it seemed to him that the enemy were surely being driven to cross the river, instead of being prevented from doing so. General Meade's message closed with these words: "It is my intention to attack the enemy tomorrow, unless something intervenes to prevent it; for delay will strengthen the enemy and will not increase my force." Calling me again to the map, and pointing out the position of the various portions of the army as he understood them . . . [Mr. Lincoln] paced the room, wringing his hands and saying: "They will be ready to fight a magnificent battle when there is no enemy to fight." His apprehensions were proved to be justifiable; for the next morning, when the attack was proposed to be made, the enemy had indeed escaped across the river. . . .

From "Lincoln and the Telegrapher" by Albert Chandler in American Heritage, *April 1961, Vol. XI No. 3 (American Heritage Publishing Co.).*

Comprehension

1. What does the first paragraph tell about Lincoln?
2. What does the last paragraph tell about Lincoln's opinion of General Meade?

Critical Thinking

3. What seems to be Chandler's opinion of Mr. Lincoln?
4. Does the information in the last paragraph match what you have read in your text? Explain your answer.

Name _____   Date _____

WORSHEET 19
Norah A. Perez, *The Slopes of War*

Norah Perez is the author of several historical novels. After visiting the national military park at Gettysburg, Pennsylvania, with her family, Perez decided to write a book about the Battle of Gettysburg. The result was *The Slopes of War,* which describes the epic battle and its effect on the people of Gettysburg. Below is a passage from the novel, told from the viewpoint of the Confederate commander, Robert E. Lee.

At Chambersburg General Lee tried to make sense out of the reports coming in to him. On Tuesday Pettigrew's men had headed into Gettysburg to find some desperately needed shoes; they had seen a few enemy uniforms and had reported back to General Heth. Convinced that what they had seen was probably the local militia, Heth had agreed to let Pettigrew return for the shoes the next morning. That was how it had started. Now a little skirmish had developed into something bigger.

As he pressed Traveller [Lee's horse] to reach Gettysburg quickly, Lee hoped that the Old Soldier's Disease, which was draining his energy, wouldn't be a nuisance to him much longer. He was feeling his age these days. It was as if his body, once fit and healthy and uncomplaining, nagged him for attention. First the heart and the troubling shortness of breath, and then this annoying dysentery. It worried him not to be in peak condition. A victory here and it was possible the war might end.

A. P. Hill, the commander of the Third Corps, was waiting, his bearded face blotched with red, twitching nervously above the collar of the crimson shirt he liked to wear into battle. He admitted that the brigades had met some surprising resistance on their shopping trip to town that morning. "But I have another division ready to go in and back up Heth. Dorsey Pender's men . . . good fellows." Hill was usually unsettled during military operations, but on this bright July morning Lee thought the man really looked quite ill as he repeated that he had men ready to go in. "With your permission, sir."

"Wait. Wait. . . . " Lee would not be rushed into this. He moved to and fro on his horse, listening to the familiar crack of muskets and the steady rumble of artillery, straining to understand what lay behind it. Heavy casualty reports were coming in now, and word had arrived that General Archer had been taken prisoner. In spite of his composure [calmness] a hot cone of anger against his cavalry burned in his chest. No, he was not angry with them, but with his favorite, Jeb Stuart, the officer who had let him down. He had known that the marvelous man had flaws, that he was sometimes too buoyant and reckless, but this time he was unforgivably late, and Lee felt like a blinded man. He did not know what the danger was or where it was located. For all he knew, the soldiers scrambling through the woods and fields northwest of town might be involved with the whole Army of the Potomac. A spy had reported columns of the enemy in the area, but he knew he wasn't ready yet for a major encounter, not until all of his troops had arrived.

Hill said, "Just give me the word, sir. Pender will clear the road for us in no time."

"Not yet." The general never minded taking risks when he had to, but he refused to be stupid. "Let's wait and see just what it is we're up against."

And so a lull occurred, a little yawn in time, even as the snap of musketry went on and shells continued to burst and blossom white against the innocent blue sky. Time for parched [thirsty] soldiers to swallow tepid water and exhausted gun crews to reposition batteries and replenish ammunition, as a long slow scarf of yellow smoke drifted across the damaged ground.

Then, abruptly, things began to happen again. The murky puzzle that was baffling Lee came together sharply with a sudden shape and clear design. Five brigades of Rodes's division appeared north of the pike on Oak Hill in exactly the right position to swoop down on the tired blue troops that faced the west. If Pender drove in now with his fresh supports, and Rodes's men slammed down hard from the hill, the Union line would have to give. Integral parts clicked smoothly into place as if they had been planned. General Lee, his instincts for opportunity humming, gave the orders.

Yet Federal gears were whirring, too. The Eleventh Corps had just arrived, men fresh for battle hurrying double-quick along the pike and fanning out north of town. It was a hard luck unit, the scapegoat of the army because of its large number of immigrant recruits, but this time it was fortunate. The Confederates rushing down from Oak Hill came too fast, too eagerly, and the Eleventh hurled them back and forced them to regroup. Now the war machine boomed heavily across the landscape, knocking down fence rails, blasting wildflowers, smashing thousands of men under as it rumbled through the sultry summer afternoon.

From The Slopes of War *by N. A. Perez. Copyright ©* *1954 by N. A. Perez. Published by Houghton Mifflin Company.*

Critical Thinking

1. Why had Confederate troops gone into Gettysburg in the first place?
2. Why was Lee upset with Jeb Stuart? What did he need Stuart to do for him?
3. When did Lee finally give the orders for his troops to attack?

Connecting History and Literature

Answer one question with a brief essay.

A. Why had Lee taken his army northward into Pennsylvania?
B. What was the outcome of the Battle of Gettysburg?

WORKSHEET 20
Life for Freed Slaves

Henry Adams was a slave on a Louisiana plantation. When the Civil War ended, he was 22 years old. In a report to the United States Senate in 1880, Adams described conditions in the South right after the war.

The white men read a paper to all of us colored people telling us that we were free and could go where we pleased and work for who we pleased. The man I belonged to told me it was best to stay with him. He said, "The bad white men was mad with the Negroes because they were free and they would kill you all for fun." He said, stay where we are living and we could get protection from our old masters.

I told him I thought that every man, when he was free, could have his rights and protect themselves. He said, "The colored people could never protect themselves among the white people. So you had all better stay with the white people who raised you and make contracts with them to work by the year. . . . We have contracts for you all to sign. . . ."

I told him I would not sign anything. I said, "I might sign to be killed. I believe the white people is trying to fool us." But he said again, "Sign this contract so I can take it to the Yankees and have it recorded." All our colored people signed it but myself and a boy named Samuel Jefferson. . . .

On the day after all had signed the contracts, we went to cutting oats. I asked the boss, "Could we get any of the oats?" He said,

"No the oats were made before you were free." After that he told us to get timber to build a sugarmill to make molasses. We did so. . . . We made two or three hundred gallons of molasses and only got what we could eat. . . . We split rails three or four weeks and got not a cent for that.

In September I asked the boss to let me go to Shreveport. He said, "All right, when will you come back?" I told him "next week." He said, "You had better carry a pass." I said, "I will see whether I am free by going without a pass."

I met four white men about six miles south of Keachie, De Soto Parish. One of them asked me who I belonged to. I told him no one. So him and two others struck me with a stick and told me they were going to kill me and every other Negro who told them that they did not belong to anyone. . . . They left me and I then went on to Shreveport. I seen over twelve colored men and women, beat, shot, and hung between there and Shreveport. . . .

From U.S. Senate Report 693, 46th Congress, 2nd Session (December 1879–June 1880). Quoted in The Trouble They Seen, *edited by Dorothy Sterling (Doubleday & Company, Inc., 1976).*

Comprehension

1. In what ways did Henry Adams's former master try to take advantage of his former slaves?
2. Why did Adams refuse to sign his former master's contract?
3. What are examples of Adams's independent thinking and determination to hold on to his rights?

Critical Thinking

4. Based on Adams's account, what were conditions like for freed slaves in the South just after the war?
5. Why might the federal government have chosen to hear a report from Henry Adams?

WORKSHEET 20

Literature

Ellen Glasgow, *The Deliverance*

Novelist Ellen Glasgow grew up in Virginia during Reconstruction. Her realistic novels made her the first writer of the modern South. Her books described changes she had seen taking place: new styles in politics, the loss of family lands and fortunes, rivalry among social classes. *The Deliverance* shows some ironies of Reconstruction. For example, the former overseer now owns the Blake family mansion, while Christopher Blake works in the tobacco fields his family once owned. In this scene, Guy Carraway, a lawyer, visits Blake's shabby cottage and discovers that his elderly mother, now blind, is unaware of these changes.

From a rear chimney a dark streak of smoke was rising, but the front of the house gave no outward sign of life, and as there came no answer to his insistent knocks he [Carraway] at last ventured to open the door and pass into the narrow hall. From the first room on the right a voice spoke at his entrance, and following the sound he found himself face to face with Mrs. Blake in her massive Elizabethan chair.

"There is a stranger in the room," she said rigidly, turning her sightless eyes; "speak at once."

"I beg pardon most humbly for my intrusion," replied Carraway, conscious of stammering like an offending schoolboy, "but as no one answered my knock, I committed the indiscretion of opening a closed door."

Awed as much by the stricken pallor [paleness] of her appearance as by the inappropriate grandeur of her black brocade and her thread lace cap, he advanced slowly and stood awaiting his dismissal.

"What door?" she demanded sharply, much to his surprise.

"Yours, madam."

"Not answer your knock?" she pursued, with indignation. "So that was the noise I heard, and no wonder that you entered. Why, what is the matter with the place? Where are the servants?"

He humbly replied that he had seen none, to be taken up with her accustomed quickness of touch.

"Seen none! Why, there are three hundred of them, sir. . . . I don't think I ever had the pleasure of meeting a Carraway before."

"That is more than probable, ma'am, but I have the advantage of you, since, as a child, I was once taken out upon the street corner merely to see you go by on your way to a fancy ball, where you appeared as Diana." . . .

"It was more than fifty years ago," murmured the old lady. . . . "The present is a very little part of life, sir; it's the past in which we store our treasures."

"You're right, you're right," replied Carraway, drawing his chair nearer the embroidered ottoman and leaning over to stroke the yellow cat; "and I'm glad to hear so cheerful a philosophy from your lips."

"It is based on a cheerful experience—I've been as you see me now only twenty years."

Only twenty years! He looked mutely round the soiled whitewashed walls, where hung a noble gathering of Blake portraits in massive old gilt frames. . . .

"Life has its trials, of course," pursued Mrs. Blake, as if speaking to herself. "I can't look out upon the June flowers, you know, and though the pink crape-myrtle at my window is in full bloom I cannot see it."

Following her gesture, Carraway glanced out into the little yard; no myrtle was there, but he remembered vaguely that he had seen one in blossom at the Hall.

"You keep flowers about you, though," he said, alluding to the scattered vases of June roses.

"Not my crape-myrtle. I planted it myself when I first came home with Mr. Blake, and

I have never allowed so much as a spray of it to be plucked."

. . . Recalling herself suddenly, her tone took on a sprightliness like that of youth.

"It's not often that we have the pleasure of entertaining a stranger in our out-of-the-way house, sir—so may I ask where you are staying—or perhaps you will do us the honour to sleep beneath our roof. It has had the privilege of sheltering General Washington."

"You are very kind," replied Carraway . . . "but to tell the truth, I feel that I am sailing under false colours. The real object of my visit is to ask a business interview with your son. I bring what seems to me a very fair offer for the place."

Grasping the carved arms of her chair, Mrs. Blake turned the wonder in her blind eyes upon him.

"An offer for the place! Why, you must be dreaming, sir! A Blake owned it more than a hundred years before the Revolution."

At the instant, understanding broke upon Carraway like a thundercloud, and as he rose from his seat it seemed to him that he had missed by a single step the yawning gulf before him. . . . He looked up to meet, from the threshold of the adjoining room, the enraged flash of Christopher's eyes. So tempestuous was the glance that Carraway . . . squared himself to receive a physical blow; but the young man . . . came in quietly and took his stand behind the Elizabethan chair.

"Why, what a joke, mother," he said, laughing; "he means the old Weatherby farm, of course. The one I wanted to sell last year, you know."

"I thought you'd sold it to the Weatherbys, Christopher."

"Not a bit of it—they backed out at the last; but don't begin to bother your head about such things; they aren't worth it. And now, sir," he turned upon Carraway, "since your business is with me, perhaps you will have the goodness to step outside."

With the feeling that he was asked out for a beating, Carraway turned for a farewell with Mrs. Blake. . . .

"Business may come later, my son," she said, detaining them by a gesture of her heavily ringed hand. "After dinner you may take Mr. Carraway with you into the library . . . ; meanwhile, he and I will resume our very pleasant talk which you interrupted. He remembers seeing me in the old days when we were all in the United States, my dear."

Christopher's brow grew black, and he threw a sharp and malignant glance of sullen suspicion at Carraway, who summoned to meet it his most frank and open look. . . .

"You may assure yourself," he [said] softly, "that I have her welfare very decidedly at heart."

At this Christopher smiled back at him. . . .

"Well, take care, sir," he answered and went out . . . while Carraway applied himself to a determined entertaining of Mrs. Blake.

To accomplish this he found that he had only to leave her free, guiding her thoughts with his lightest touch into newer channels. . . . Everywhere he felt her wonderful keenness of perception—that intuitive understanding of men and manners which had kept her for so long the reigning belle among her younger rivals.

As she went on he found that her world was as different from his own as if she dwelt upon some undiscovered planet. . . . She lived upon lies, he saw, and thrived upon the sweetness she extracted from them. For her the Confederacy had never fallen, the quiet of her dreamland had been disturbed by no invading army, and the three hundred slaves, who had in reality scattered like chaff before the wind, she still saw in her cheerful visions tilling her familiar fields. It was as if she had fallen asleep with the great blow that had wrecked her body, and had dreamed on steadily throughout the years. . . . In her memory there was no Appomattox, news of the death of Lincoln had never reached her ears, and president had peacefully succeeded president in the secure Confederacy in which she lived. Wonderful as it all was, to Carraway the most wonderful thing was the intricate tissue of lies woven around her chair. Lies—lies—there had been nothing but lies spoken within her hearing for twenty years.

From The Deliverance, *by Ellen Glasgow (Doubleday, Page & Co., 1904).*

Critical Thinking

1. What clues are given to the Blake family's former wealth?
2. What did Mrs. Blake mean when she referred to "the old days when we were all in the United States"?
3. What did Mrs. Blake believe was the outcome of the Civil War?

Connecting History and Literature

Answer one question with a brief essay.

A. In what important was was the postwar South different from the prewar South?

B. Would a northerner after the Civil War have behaved toward Mrs. Blake in the same way that Carraway, a southern lawyer, did? Why or why not?

WORKSHEET 21
Distributing Private Wealth

Primary Source

By the late 1880s, criticism of the private ownership of immense wealth had begun to surface in American society. To defend the acquisition of large sums of money in a capitalist society, Andrew Carnegie wrote the article "Wealth" in 1889. Following are excerpts from his article.

Upon the sacredness of property civilization itself depends—the right of the laborer to his hundred dollars in the savings bank, and equally the legal right of the millionaire to his millions. . . .

We start, then, with a condition of affairs under which the best interests of the race are promoted, but which inevitably gives wealth to the few. Thus far, accepting conditions as they exist, the situation can be surveyed and pronounced good. The question then arises— . . . What is the proper mode of administering wealth after the laws upon which civilization is founded have thrown it into the hands of the few? And it is of this great question that I believe I offer the true solution. . . .

There are but three modes in which surplus wealth can be disposed of. It can be left to the families of the decedents; or it can be bequeathed for public purposes; or finally, it can be administered during their lives by its possessors. . . . Observation teaches that, generally speaking, it is not well for the children that they should be so burdened. . . . Beyond providing for the wife and daughters moderate sources of income, and very moderate allowances indeed, if any, for the sons, men may well hesitate, for it is no longer questionable that great sums bequeathed often work more for the injury than for the good of the recipients. . . .

As to the second mode, that of leaving wealth at death for public uses, it may be said that this is only a means for the disposal of wealth, provided a man is content to wait until he is dead before he becomes of much good in the world. . . .

There remains, then, only one mode of using great fortunes; but in this we have the true antidote for the temporary unequal distribution of wealth, the reconciliation of the rich and the poor. . . . Under its sway we shall have an ideal state, in which the surplus wealth of the few will become, in the best sense, the property of the many, because administered for the common good; and this wealth, passing through the hands of the few, can be made a much more potent force for the elevation of our race that if it had been distributed in small sums to the people themselves. . . .

From "Wealth," by Andrew Carnegie in North American Review *(June, 1889). Quoted in* Great Issues in American History, A Documentary Record, Vol. II, *edited by Richard Hofstadter (Vintage Books, 1958).*

Comprehension

1. According to Carnegie, in what three ways could people dispose of their wealth?
2. Which way does Carnegie prefer? Why?
3. Why did Carnegie think it was not a good idea to leave large sums of money to family members?

Critical Thinking

4. In his lifetime, did Carnegie take his own advice? Explain your answer, using your textbook as needed.
5. Why might Carnegie's ideas appeal to wealthy people?
6. What are some possible arguments against Carnegie's position?

Name _____ Date _____

WORKSHEET 21 Literature
William Dean Howells, *A Hazard of New Fortunes*

Despite the rise of organized labor and the labor unrest of the late 1800s, few mainstream American authors before the 1930s wrote about the union movement. William Dean Howells's A *Hazard of New Fortunes* is unusual even for this realist author. Published in 1890, his novel presents urban social problems as they affect a variety of contrasting characters. Their reactions to a New York City streetcar strike differ dramatically. Although Howells shaped the material to fit his plot, he based the incident on an actual 1889 strike. In this scene, the idealistic Conrad Dryfoos confronts his father, a wealthy magazine publisher who is also angry with Conrad's sister Christine.

He [the elder Dryfoos] took the elevated road [train]. The strike seemed a very far-off thing, though the paper he bought to look up the stock market was full of noisy typography about yesterday's troubles on the surface lines. Among the millionaires in Wall Street there was some joking and some swearing, but not much thinking about the six thousand men who had taken such chances in their attempt to better their condition. Dryfoos heard nothing of the strike in the lobby of the Stock Exchange, where he spent two or three hours watching a favorite stock of his go up and go down under the betting. By the time the Exchange closed it had risen eight points, and on this and some other investments he was five thousand dollars richer than he had been in the morning. But he had expected to be richer still, and he was by no means satisfied with his luck. All through the excitement of his winning and losing had played the dull, murderous rage he felt toward the child [his daughter] who had defied him, and when the game was over and he started home, his rage mounted into a sort of frenzy; he would teach her, he would break her. He walked a long way without thinking, and then waited for a car [streetcar]. None came, and he hailed a passing coupé [horse-drawn carriage].

"What has got all the cars?" he demanded of the driver, who jumped down from his box to open the door for him and get his direction.

"Been away?" asked the driver. "Hasn't

been any car along for a week. Strike."

"Oh yes," said Dryfoos. He felt suddenly giddy, and he remained staring at the driver after he had taken his seat.

The man asked, "Where to?"

Dryfoos could not think of his street or number, and he said, with uncontrollable fury: "I told you once! Go up to West Eleventh, and drive along slow on the south side; I'll show you the place."

He could not remember the number of *Every Other Week* [his magazine office], where he suddenly decided to stop before he went home. . . .

There was nobody but Conrad in the counting-room, whither Dryfoos returned after glancing into Fulkerson's empty office. . . .

"Do you generally knock off here in the middle of the afternoon?" asked the old man.

"No," said Conrad, as patiently as if his father had not been there a score of times and found the whole staff of *Every Other Week* at work between four and five. "Mr. March, you know, takes a good deal of his work home with him, and I suppose Mr. Fulkerson went out so early because there isn't much doing to-day. Perhaps it's the strike that makes it dull."

"The strike—yes! It's a pretty piece of business to have everything thrown out because a parcel of lazy hounds want a chance to lay off and get drunk." Dryfoos seemed to think Conrad would make some answer to this, but the young man's mild face merely saddened, and he said nothing. "I've got a coupé out there now that I had to take because I couldn't get a car. If I had my way I'd have a lot of those vagabonds hung. They're waiting to get the city into a snarl, and then rob the houses—pack of dirty worthless whelps. They ought to call out the militia, and fire into'em. Clubbing is too good for them." Conrad was still silent, and his father sneered, "But I reckon *you* don't think so."

"I think the strike is useless," said Conrad.

"Oh, you *do*, do you? Comin' to your senses a little. Gettin' tired walkin' so much. . . ."

"Father, you know we don't agree about these things. I'd rather not talk—"

"But I'm goin' to *make* you talk this time!" cried Dryfoos, striking the arm of the chair he sat in with the side of his fist. A maddening thought of Christine came over him. "As long as you eat my bread, you have got to do as I say. I won't have my children telling me what I shall do and sha'n't do, or take on airs of being holier than me. Now, you just speak up! Do you think those loafers are right, or don't you? Come!"

Conrad apparently judged it best to speak. "I think they were very foolish to strike—at this time, when the elevated roads can do the work."

"Oh, at this time, heigh! And I suppose they think over there on the east side that it'd been wise to strike before we got the elevated?" Conrad again refused to answer, and his father roared, "What do you think?"

"I think a strike is always bad business. It's war; but sometimes there don't seem any other way for the working-men to get justice. They say that sometimes strikes do raise the wages, after a while."

"Those lazy devils were paid enough already," shrieked the old man. "They got two dollars a day. How much do you think they ought to 'a' got? Twenty?"

Conrad hesitated, with a beseeching look at his father. But he decided to answer. "The men say that with partial work, and fines, and other things, they get sometimes a dollar, and some times ninety cents a day."

"They lie, and you *know* they lie," said his father, rising and coming toward him. "And what do you think the upshot of it all will be, after they've ruined business for another week, and made people hire hacks, and stolen the money of honest men? How is it going to end?"

"They will have to give in."

"Oh, give in, heigh! And what will you say *then*, I should like to know? How will you feel about it then? Speak!"

"I shall feel as I do now. I know you don't think that way, and I don't blame you—or any body. But if I have got to say how I shall feel, why, I shall feel sorry they didn't succeed, for I believe they have a righteous cause, though they go the wrong way to help themselves."

His father came close to him, his eyes blazing, his teeth set. "Do you *dare* to say that to me?"

"Yes. I can't help it. I pity them; my whole heart is with those poor men."

"You impudent puppy!" shouted the old man. He lifted his hand and struck his son in the face. Conrad caught his hand with his own left, and while the blood began to trickle from a wound that [the] intaglio ring had made in his temple, he looked at him with a kind of grieving wonder, and said, "Father!"

From A Hazard of New Fortunes, *by William Dean Howells (Harper & Brothers, 1890).*

Critical Thinking

1. What clues in the opening paragraphs suggest that Howells was sympathetic to the strikers' aims?
2. What are Conrad's reasons for thinking the strike was a mistake?
3. What techniques does Howells use to make this scene seem realistic?

Connecting History and Literature

Answer one question with a brief essay.

A. Why were there growing conflicts between workers and owners in the second half of the 1800s?
B. During this period, what was the government's attitude toward strikes?

WORSHEET 22
Government in the Cities

Primary Source

WORKSHEET 22
Government in the Cities

Lincoln Steffens, an editor for *McClure's Magazine,* traveled to over a dozen cities in 1902 and 1903. As a result of his travels, he wrote a series of articles about municipal corruption. These articles appeared first in his magazine, and then in 1904 they were published as a book, *The Shame of the Cities.* Following are excerpts from his book.

Tammany is bad government; not inefficient, but dishonest; . . . Tammany is for Tammany, and the Tammany men say so. . . . Tammany is honestly dishonest. Time and time again, in private and in public, the leaders, big and little, have said they are out for themselves and their own; not for the public, but for "me and my friends"; not for New York, but for Tammany. . . .

Tammany's democratic corruption rests upon the corruption of the people, the plain people, and there lies its great significance; its grafting system is one in which more individuals share than any I have studied. The people themselves get very little; they come cheap, but they are interested. Divided into districts, the organization subdivides them into precincts or neighborhoods, and their sovereign power, in the form of votes, is bought up by kindness and petty privileges. They are forced to a surrender, when neces-

sary, by intimidation, but the leader and his captains have their hold because they take care of their own. . . .

Tammany leaders are usually the natural leaders of the people in these districts, and they are originally good-natured, kindly men. . . . Their charity is real, at first. But they sell out their own people. They do give them coal and help them in their private troubles, but, as they grow rich and powerful, the kindness goes out of the charity and they not only collect at their saloons or in rents—cash for their "goodness"; . . . they sacrifice the children in the schools; let the Health Department neglect the tenements, and, worst of all, plant vice in the neighborhood and in homes of the poor.

From The Shame of the Cities, *by Lincoln Steffens (New York: McClure, Phillips and Company, 1904).*

Comprehension

1. In the second paragraph, what criticisms does Steffens have of the Tammany bosses?
2. What positive remarks does Steffens make in describing the Tammany bosses?
3. In the third paragraph, what criticism does Steffens make of the Tammany bosses?

Critical Thinking

4. In the late 1800s, where had many of the people living in cities come from? How would this fact likely have affected reaction to Tammany bosses?
5. Which do you think Steffens thought was more important—honest government or giving a helping hand to people in need? Why?

Name _____   Date _____

WORKSHEET 22
Sholem Asch, Summer in New York

Nearly all the European immigrants of the late 1800s arrived first in New
York City, and many settled there. In his book *East River,* Sholem Asch
describes life in an immigrant neighborhood on 48th Street.

The evening brought no relief from the oppressive heat. On the contrary, the walls of the buildings, having absorbed the heat all day, now began to throw it back into the street. The air was so humid that the people of the neighborhood had the feeling they were wrapped in a damp sheet which hampered their movements and from which they were unable to free themselves. It was impossible to stay indoors. The walls, the ceilings, the floors sweated with heat; the dampness filled the rooms and made it impossible to breathe. The heavy smells of food, sweat, and clothing, and the stale smell of mattresses and bedclothes added to the oppressiveness. The heat seemed to make bodies enormous and cumbersome. It sapped the energy and tortured the limbs.

The block dwellers swarmed out of their rooms, searching for a relieving gust of air. They crowded the fire escapes, the steps in front of doors, and the sidewalks.

Most of all they sought relief in the cool winds that came once in a while over the East River. But direct approach to the river shore was blocked to them. The streets ended in "dead ends" hemmed in by fences erected by the owners of the feed storehouses and stables. In a couple of places, however, there was an old unused dock, the planks water-soaked and rotted. From these docks one could hear the splashing of children swimming close to the shore, driven to find relief from the overpowering heat, disregarding the perils of the holes and falling timbers of the dock.

Other entrances to the waterfront were provided by the stables on the river shore. By climbing over fences and scrambling over the stable roofs it was possible to get down to the water's edge.

But 48th Street had two yards that opened on the river, and of these the people of the adjoining blocks were properly jealous. One of them was Harry's, to which, naturally, only his intimate friends, the people of his own block, who were interested in his pigeons, had admission. The other belonged to a private real-estate firm. Tammany [a political machine] had taken over the use of it so that the legitimate dwellers on 48th Street could come there to take their ease on the hot summer nights. With Judge Greenberg's help Uncle Maloney had managed to get permission to keep the property open to the Tammany members in the block. There was a lot of competition for the privilege among the inhabitants of the street. The yard stretched to the river shore, and the general belief was that cool winds blew there. Everyone in the neighborhood besieged the office of the Tammany captain for tickets of admission. The first tickets, naturally enough, went to the members in good standing of the local Tammany club; Maloney knew all of them. But in time everyone on the block came to feel that he or she had special rights to the place, even Heimowitz, the socialist, who had little enough to do with Tammany in other matters. The yard was full of people; men, women, and children of the neighborhood. They had brought with them mattresses, blankets, pillows, cans of cold tea or beer or ice water, ready to spend half the night there, until the tenement rooms got cool enough to return to.

The river lay motionless in its broad bed, its dark patches of oily scum reflecting the star-studded sky. Now and then a light blinked from a slowly moving coal barge. A heavy silence lay over the river.

From time to time the hoarse blast of a freight boat cut through the air. The morbid prison shadows of Blackwell's Island in the middle of the river pressed on the water's surface. The dimly lighted mist that hung over the island seemed to oppress the spirit and burden the heart more than it served to lighten the darkness. Involuntarily, everyone who saw the lights gleaming through the island's mist would think of the poor devils sent "across the river." The melancholy which the sight of the island brought to every one of Manhattan's dwellers fell like a pall on the group gathered in the Tammany yard to escape the unbearable heat. How could anyone of them know what the morrow might bring? Poverty ruled their lives and—who could know?—might drive them relentlessly to a similar fate. The same melancholy drove them to find escape in sleep, to find a rest from all the cares and worries of the day.

Some of them sprawled out on blankets they had brought with them from their homes. Others, the Slavs, for instance, talked with animation about the old country, about the boats that floated down its rivers; the nearness of the East River had brought it to their minds. Yes, along the Vistula, the Bug, and the Volga enormous rafts of logs floated; people would live on them all summer. They talked about horses being led in the night to graze on the green plains.

"Another year's work in the slaughterhouse, and I'll save enough, and then back home, back to Czezov. I'll buy my brother's share and take over my father's farm, eight acres and ten head of cattle." Choleva let his fantasy roam. His speech was a mixture of Polish, Russian, and English.

"It'll be no good. You'll use up your few dollars in the old country and then you'll come back to America. Everybody comes back. One smell of the American air, and it draws you back. There's some kind of magic in it," someone said.

From East River *by Sholem Asch. Copyright © 1986 by Carroll & Graf Publishers.*

Critical Thinking

1. Why was it difficult for people to go to the river shore?
2. Why, do you think, did some of the people talk about returning to their home country?
3. What do you think the final speaker meant by the phrase "the American air"?

Connecting History and Literature

Answer one question with a brief essay.

A. What clues in the excerpt tell you that some of the people in this scene are from southern and eastern Europe?
B. Why, in your opinion, did people remain in crowded and uncomfortable tenements rather than move out of the city?

WORKSHEET 23
A Stampede

Primary Source

Below is an account of a stampede, written by William A. Baillie Grohman, an Englishman, and first published in 1886. Read the account. Then answer the questions that follow.

On the approach of one of these violent outbursts [a thunderstorm] the whole force is ordered on duty; the spare horses—of which each man has always three, and often as many as eight or ten—are carefully fed and tethered, and the herd is "rounded up," that is, collected into as small a space as possible, while the men continue to ride around the densely massed herd. Like horses, cattle derive courage from the close proximity of men. The thunder peals, and the vivid lightning flashes with amazing brilliancy, as with lowered heads the herd eagerly watch the slow, steady pace of the cow-ponies, and no doubt derive from it a comforting sense of protection. Sometimes, however, a wild steer will be unable to control his terror, and will make a dash through a convenient opening. The crisis is at hand, for the example will surely be followed, and in two minutes the whole herd of 4000 head will have broken through the line of horsemen and be away, one surging, bellowing mass of terrified beasts. Fancy a pitch-dark night, a pouring torrent of rain, the ground not only entirely strange to the men, but very broken, and full of dangerously steep water-courses and hollows, and you will have a picture of cow-boy duty on such a night. They must head off the leaders. Once fairly off, they will stampede twenty, thirty, and even forty miles at a stretch, and many branches will stray from the main herd. Not alone the reckless driver, but also the horses . . . are perfectly aware of how much depends upon their speed that night, if it kills them. . . .

Urged on by a shout, the horses speed alongside the terrified steers until they manage to reach the leaders, when, swinging around, and fearless of horns, they press back the bellowing brutes till they turn them. All the men pursuing this manoeuvre, the headlong rush is at last checked, and the leaders, panting and lashing their sides with their tails, are brought to a stand, and the whole herd is again "rounded up."

From "The American Cow-Boy," by Joseph Nimmo, Jr., in Harper's New Monthly Magazine *(November, 1886).*

Comprehension

1. According to the author, what is the attitude of cattle toward men?
2. What dangers do cowboys face during a stampede?
3. How do cowboys halt stampedes?

Critical Thinking

4. What is the author's point of view regarding cowboys? Explain why.
5. What personal qualities do you think a person would have needed to be a successful cowboy?

Name _____ Date _____

The Plains Indian culture depended on the buffalo. As white settlers slaughtered countless thousands of buffalo, they helped destroy the Plains Indian way of life. In this legend, Old Lady Horse (Spear Woman), a Kiowa, describes the destruction of the buffalo.

And now we come to the end of a world. The end of the buffalo was the end of Plains Indian life. And before the white man's superior technology, the buffalo succumbed. This is one story of why there are no more buffalo in the world.

Everything the Kiowas had came from the buffalo. Their tipis were made of buffalo hides, so were their clothes and moccasins. They ate buffalo meat. Their containers were made of hide, or of bladders or stomachs. The buffalo were the life of the Kiowas.

Most of all, the buffalo was part of the Kiowa religion. A white buffalo calf must be sacrificed in the Sun Dance. The priests used parts of the buffalo to make their prayers when they healed people or when they sang to the powers above.

So, when the white men wanted to build railroads, or when they wanted to farm or raise cattle, the buffalo still protected the Kiowas. They tore up the railroad tracks and the gardens. They chased the cattle off the ranges. The buffalo loved their people as much as the Kiowas loved them.

There was war between the buffalo and the white men. The white men built forts in the Kiowa country, and . . . shot the buffalo as fast as they could, but the buffalo kept coming on, coming on, even into the post cemetery at Fort Sill. Soldiers were not enough to hold them back.

Then the white men hired hunters to do nothing but kill the buffalo. Up and down the plains those men ranged, shooting sometimes as many as a hundred buffalo a day. Behind them came the skinners with their wagons. They piled the hides and bones into the wagons until they were full, and then took their loads to the new railroad stations that were being built, to be shipped east to the market. Sometimes there would be a pile of bones as high as a man, stretching a mile along the railroad track.

The buffalo saw that their day was over. They could protect their people no longer. Sadly, the last remnant of the great herd gathered in council, and decided what they would do.

The Kiowas were camped on the north side of Mount Scott, those of them who were still free to camp. One young woman got up very early in the morning. The dawn mist was still rising from Medicine Creek, and as she looked across the water, peering through the haze, she saw the last buffalo herd appear like a spirit dream.

Straight to Mount Scott the leader of the herd walked. Behind him came the cows and their calves, and the few young males who had survived. As the woman watched, the face of the mountain opened.

Inside Mount Scott the world was green and fresh, as it had been when she was a small girl. The rivers ran clear, not red. The wild plums were in blossom, chasing the red buds up the inside slopes. Into this world of beauty the buffalo walked never to be seen again.

"End of The World: The Buffalo Go" as told to Alice Marriott by Old Lady Horse (Spear Woman), Kiowa. From American Indian Mythology, *Alice Marriott and Carol K. Rachlin, Editors. Copyright © 1968 by Alice Marriott and Carol K. Rachlin*

Critical Thinking

1. Describe the different uses the Kiowas made of the buffalo.
2. In what ways did the buffalo protect the Kiowas?
3. The story ends with the buffalo entering the mountain. What might be the symbolic importance of this ending?

Connecting History and Literature

Answer one question with a brief essay.

A. The Kiowas killed buffalo for their hides and meat, yet this story portrays the Kiowas and the buffalo as allies. Explain why this is so.
B. Explain the following statement by an army officer, quoted in your textbook: "Every buffalo dead is an Indian gone."

WORKSHEET 24
The Farmers' Plight

Primary Source

In the late 1800s, the economic position of American farmers worsened. Washington Gladden, an influential Congregational minister, preached the application of religious principles to social problems. In a magazine article written in 1890, Gladden described the plight of farmers.

The farmers of the United States are up in arms. They are the bone and sinew of the nation; they produce the largest share of its wealth; but they are getting, they say, the smallest share for themselves. The American farmer is steadily losing ground. His burdens are heavier every year and his gains are more meager; he is beginning to fear that he may be sinking into a servile condition. He has waited long for the redress of his grievances; he [intends] to wait no longer. Whatever he can do by social combinations or by united political action to remove the disabilities under which he is suffering, he intends to do at once and with all his might.

There is no doubt at all that the farmers of this country are tremendously in earnest just now, and they have reason to be. Beyond question they are suffering sorely. The business of farming has become, for some reasons, extremely unprofitable. With the hardest work and with the sharpest economy, the average farmer is unable to make both ends meet; every year closes with debt, and the mortgage grows till it devours the land. The Labor Bureau of Connecticut has shown, by an investigation of 693 represen-

tative farms, that the average annual reward of the farm proprietor of that state for his expenditure of muscle and brain is $181.31, while the average annual wages of the ordinary hired man is $386.36. Even if the price of board must come out of the hired man's [wages], is still leaves him a long way ahead of his employer. . . .

In Ohio, farms are offered for beggarly rents, and even on these favorable terms farming does not pay. Tenant farmers are throwing up their leases and moving into the cities, well content to receive as common laborers $1.25 a day, and to pay such rents and to run such risks of enforced idleness as the change involves. At the South the case is even worse. Under a heavy burden of debt the farmer struggles on from year to year, the phenomenal growth of the manufacturing interests in his section seeming to bring him but slight relief. And even in the West we find the same state of things. . . . From Kansas and Nebraska and Dakota the cry is no less loud and bitter. . . .

From "The Embattled Farmers," by Washington Gladden in Forum, *Vol. 10 (November 1890).*

Comprehension

1. What difficulties faced the American farmer, according to Reverend Gladden?
2. In what parts of the United States were farmers suffering hardship?
3. What actions were American farmers taking to overcome these problems?

Critical Thinking

4. What were some of the reasons for the plight of the farmers? Use your textbook as needed to answer this question.
5. What actions did farmers take to help their situation? Use your textbook as needed to answer this question.

Name _____   Date _____

Lincoln Steffens, "Boy on Horseback"

Lincoln Steffens was one of the progressive era's best known investigative journalists—the writers whom Theodore Roosevelt called "muckrakers." As an editor and reporter, he uncovered political corruption and worked actively for reform. Steffens's autobiography (1931) recounts his long and influential career. The first section, "Boy on Horseback," tells about his childhood in Sacramento, California. This excerpt describes how Steffens, as a teenager in the 1880s, first became aware of politics when his friend Charlie Marple got a job as a page (carrying messages and running errands) in the California legislature.

I saw that the Legislature wasn't what my father, my teachers, and the grown-ups thought; it wasn't even what my histories and the other books said. There was some mystery about it as there was about art, as there was about everything. Nothing was what it was supposed to be. . . .

I enjoyed the sessions of the House when Charlie had to be on the floor. He found me a seat just back of the rail where I could sit and watch him and the other pages running about among the legislators in their seats. Charlie used to stand beside me, he and the other small pages, between calls, and we learned the procedure. We became expert on the rules. The practices of debate, quite aside from the legislation under consideration, fascinated me. I wished it were real. It was beautiful enough to be true. But no, speeches were made on important subjects with hardly anyone present but the Speaker, the clerks, and us boys. Where were the absent members? I did not ask that question often; not out loud. The pages laughed; everybody laughed. Charlie explained.

"The members are out where the fate of the measure debated here is being settled," and he took me to committee rooms and hotel apartments where, with the drinks and cigars, members were playing poker with the lobbyists and leaders. "The members against the bill are allowed to win the price agreed on to buy their vote."

Bribery! I might as well have been shot. Somewhere in my head or my heart I was wounded deeply.

Once, when the Speaker was not in the chair and many members were in their seats, when there was a dead debate in an atmosphere of great tension, I was taken down a corridor to the closed door of a committee room. There stood reporters and a small crowd of others watching outside. We waited awhile till, at last, the Speaker came out, said something, and hurried with the crowd back to the Assembly. Charlie held me back to point out to me "the big bosses" who had come "up the river" to "force that bill through"; they had "put on the screws." I was struck by the observation that one of the bosses was blind. We went back to the House, and quickly, after a very ordinary debate of hours, the bill was passed on the third reading and sent to the Senate, where in due course it was approved. It was a "rotten deal," the boys said, and I remember my father shook his head over it. "The rascals," he muttered.

And that, so far as I could make out from him and from all witnesses—that was the explanation. The Legislature, government—everything was "all right," only there were some "bad men" who spoiled things—now and then. "Politicians" they were called, those bad men. How I hated them, in the abstract. In the concrete—I saw Charlie Prodger often in the lobby of the Legislature, and I remember that someone said he was "one of them," a "politician." But I knew Charlie Prodger; and I knew he was not a "bad man." . . .

Why didn't somebody challenge the rascals—if they were so bad? The boss of Sacramento, Frank Rhodes, the gambler, was having one of his conventions of the local ringleaders in a room under his gambling-house. It was at night. There were no outsiders present, none wanted, and the insiders were fighting, shooting men. During the meeting Grove L. Johnson, a well-known attorney in the town, walked in with his two sons, Albert and Hiram, both little more than boys, and both carrying revolvers. They went up to the front, and with one of his boys on one side of him, the other on the other, Mr. Johnson told those crooks all about themselves and what they were doing. He was bitter, fearless, free-spoken; he insulted, he defied [openly opposed] those politicians; he called upon the town to clean them out and predicted that their power would be broken some day. There was no answer. When he had finished, he and his sons walked out. . . .

What struck and stunned me at the time was that this courageous attack by the Johnsons—especially by the boys—had no effect upon the people I knew. I was trying to see the Legislature and the government as Mr. Marple [Charlie's father, a painter] saw the sunset through the brush in the river bottom; not the mud but—the gold, the Indians—some beauty in them. The painter said there always was something beautiful to see. Well, Mr. Johnson and his two boys—their defiance was beautiful; wasn't it? I thought so, and yet nobody else did. Why? I gave it up, or, better, I laid the question aside. I had other things to think of, wonderful things, things more in my line.

From Boy on Horseback *by Lincoln Steffens. Copyright 1931, 1935 by Harcourt, Brace and Company. Reprinted by permission of Harcourt Brace.*

Critical Thinking

1. What ideals about government did young Steffens hold? How did his first encounters with politics shake them?
2. What problem did Steffens have with the difference between his abstract dislike of politicians as "bad men" and his feelings for the real people he met?
3. How did the political situation in Sacramento help inspire the career of Steffens?

Connecting History and Literature

Answer one question with a brief essay.

A. In what ways can journalists be a force for reform?
B. In what different areas did progressives have an impact?

WORSHEET 25
Woodrow Wilson's War Message

Primary Source

President Woodrow Wilson avoided entry into World War I during his first administration. However, when German submarines sank several American merchant ships in March 1917, Wilson asked Congress for a declaration of war. Following are excerpts from his speech to Congress on April 2.

The new [German] policy has swept every restriction aside. Vessels of every kind . . . have been ruthlessly sent to the bottom without warning and without thought of help or mercy for those on board. . . . The present German submarine warfare . . . is a war against all nations. . . . Our motive will not be revenge or the victorious assertion of the physical might of the nation, but only the vindication of right, of human right. . . . We are . . . the sincere friends of the German people. . . . We shall, happily, still have an opportunity to prove that friendship in our daily attitude and actions towards the millions of men and women of German birth and native sympathy who live amongst us and share our life. . . .

There are . . . many months of fiery trial and sacrifice ahead of us. It is a fearful thing to lead this great peaceful people into war, into the most terrible and disastrous of all wars, civilization itself seeming to be in the balance. But the right is more precious than peace, and we shall fight for the things which we have always carried nearest our hearts,—for democracy, for the right of those who submit to authority to have a voice in their own Governments, for the rights and liberties of small nations, for a universal dominion of right . . . as shall bring peace and safety to all nations and make the world itself at last free. To such a task we can dedicate our lives and our fortunes, everything that we are and everything that we have, with the pride of those who know that the day has come when America is privileged to spend her blood and her might for the principles that gave her birth and happiness and the peace which she has treasured. . . .

From Woodrow Wilson's address to a Joint Session of the Two Houses of Congress, U.S. Senate Document 5, 65th Congress, 1st Session (April 2, 1917).

Comprehension

1. What persuaded President Wilson to seek a declaration of war against Germany?
2. What motive did Wilson express for United States participation in the war?
3. Why did Wilson reaffirm American friendship toward the German people?
4. Why was Wilson willing to lead the American people into "the most terrible and disastrous of all wars"?

Critical Thinking

5. Paraphrase the last sentence of this passage.

WORKSHEET 25
John Dos Passos, *Three Soldiers*

The death and devastation of World War I created a mood of hopelessness among many American writers. John Dos Passos had been an ambulance driver in France during the war. He began his writing career in 1921 with the realistic war novel *Three Soldiers.* In this scene, Dan Fuselli and his company get ready to ship out.

The stars were very bright when Fuselli, eyes stinging with sleep, stumbled out of the barracks. They trembled like bits of brilliant jelly in the black velvet of the sky, just as something inside him trembled with excitement.

"Anybody know where the electricity turns on?" asked the sergeant in a good-humored voice. "Here it is." The light over the door of the barracks snapped on, revealing a rotund [round] cheerful man with a little yellow mustache and an unlit cigarette dangling out of the corner of his mouth. Grouped about him, in overcoats and caps, the men of the company rested their packs against their knees.

"All right; line up, men."

Eyes looked curiously at Fuselli as he lined up with the rest. He had been transferred into the company the night before.

"Attenshun," shouted the sergeant. Then he wrinkled up his eyes and grinned hard at the slip of paper he had in his hand, while the men of his company watched him affectionately.

"Answer 'Here' when your name is called. Allan, B. C."

"Yo!" came a shrill voice from the end of the line.

"Anspach."

"Here."

Meanwhile outside the other barracks other companies could be heard calling the roll. Somewhere from the end of the street came a cheer.

"Well, I guess I can tell you now, fellers," said the sergeant with his air of quiet omniscience [complete knowledge], when he had called the last name. "We're going overseas."

Everybody cheered.

"Shut up, you don't want the Huns to hear us, do you?"

The company laughed, and there was a broad grin on the sergeant's round face.

"Seem to have a pretty decent top-kicker" whispered Fuselli to the man next to him.

"You bet yer, kid, he's a peach," said the other man in a voice full of devotion. "This is some company, I can tell you that."

"You bet it is," said the next man along. "The corporal's in the Red Sox outfield."

The lieutenant appeared suddenly in the area of light in front of the barracks. He was a pink-faced boy. His trench coat, a little too large, was very new and stuck out stiffly from his legs.

"Everything all right, sergeant? Everything all right?" he asked several times, shifting his weight from one foot to the other.

"All ready for entrainment [boarding trains], sir;" said the sergeant heartily.

"Very good, I'll let you know the order of march in a minute."

Fuselli's ears pounded with strange excitement. These phrases, "entrainment," "order of march," had a businesslike sound. He suddenly started to wonder how it would feel to be under fire. Memories of movies flickered in his mind.

"Gawd, ain't I glad to git out o' this hell-hole," he said to the man next to him.

"The next one may be more of a hell-hole yet, buddy," said the sergeant striding up and down with his important confident walk.

Everybody laughed.

"He's some sergeant, our sergeant is," said the man next to Fuselli. "He's got brains in his head, that boy has."

"All right, break ranks," said the sergeant,

"But if anybody moves away from this barracks, I'll put him in K.P. till—till he'll be able to peel spuds in his sleep."

The company laughed again. Fuselli noticed with displeasure that the tall man with the shrill voice whose name had been called first on the roll did not laugh but spat disgustedly out of the corner of his mouth.

"Well, there are bad eggs in every good bunch," thought Fuselli.

It gradually grew grey with dawn. Fuselli's legs were tired from standing so long. Outside all the barracks, as far as be could see up the street, men stood in ragged lines waiting.

The sun rose hot on a cloudless day. A few sparrows twittered about the tin roof of the barracks.

"Well, we're not goin' this day."

"Why?" asked somebody savagely.

"Troops always leaves at night. . . . Here comes Sarge."

Everybody craned their necks in the direction pointed out.

The sergeant strolled up with a mysterious smile on his face.

"Put away your overcoats and get out your mess kits."

Mess kits clattered and gleamed in the slanting rays of the sun. They marched to the mess hall and back again, lined up again with packs and waited some more.

Everybody began to get tired and peevish. Fuselli wondered where his old friends of the other company were. They were good kids too, Chris and that educated fellow, Andrews. Tough luck they couldn't have come along.

The sun rose higher. Men sneaked into the barracks one by one and lay down on the bare cots.

"What you want to bet we won't leave this camp for a week yet?" asked someone.

At noon they lined up for mess again, ate dismally and hurriedly. As Fuselli was leaving the mess hall tapping a tattoo on his kit with two dirty fingernails, the corporal spoke to him in a low voice.

"Be sure to wash yer kit, buddy. We may have pack inspection."

The corporal was a slim yellow-faced man with a wrinkled skin, though he was still young, and an arrow-shaped mouth that opened and shut like the paper mouths children make.

"All right, corporal," Fuselli answered cheerfully. He wanted to make a good impression. "Fellers'll be sayin' 'All right, corporal,' to me soon, he thought. An idea that he repelled came into his mind. The corporal didn't look strong. He wouldn't last long overseas. And he pictured Mabe [Mabel] writing Corporal Dan Fuselli, O.A.R.D.5.

At the end of the afternoon, the lieutenant appeared suddenly, his face flushed, his trench coat stiffer than ever.

"All right, sergeant; line up your men," he said in a breathless voice.

All down the camp street companies were forming. One by one they marched out in columns of fours and halted with their packs on. The day was getting amber with sunset. Retreat sounded.

Fuselli's mind had suddenly become very active. The notes of the bugle and of the band playing "The Star-Spangled Banner" sifted into his consciousness through a dream of what it would be like over there. He was in a place like the Exposition ground, full of old men and women in peasant costume, like in the song, "When It's Apple Blossom Time in Normandy." Men in spiked helmets who looked like firemen kept charging through, like the Ku-Klux Klan in the movies, jumping from their horses and setting fire to buildings with strange outlandish gestures, spitting [spearing] babies on their long swords. Those were the Huns. Then there were flags blowing very hard in the wind, and the sound of a band. The Yanks were coming. Everything was lost in a scene from a movie in which khaki-clad regiments marched fast, fast across the scene. The memory of the shouting that always accompanied it drowned out the picture. "The guns must make a racket though," he added as an after-thought.

"Atten-shun!"

"Forwa-ard, march!"

The long street of the camp was full of the tramping of feet. They were off. As they passed through the gate Fuselli caught a glimpse of Chris standing with his arm about Andrews's shoulders. They both waved. Fuselli grinned and expanded his chest. They were just rookies still. He was going overseas.

The weight of the pack tugged at his shoulders and made his feet heavy as if they were charged with lead. The sweat ran down his close-clipped head under the overseas cap and streamed into his eyes and down the sides of his nose. Through the tramp of feet he heard confusedly cheering from the sidewalk. In front of him the backs of heads and the swaying packs got smaller; rank by rank up the street. Above them flags dangled from windows, flags leisurely swaying in the twilight. But the weight of the pack, as the column marched under arc lights glaring through the afterglow, inevitably forced his head to droop forward. The soles of boots and legs wrapped in puttees and the bottom strap of the pack of the man ahead of him were all he could see. The pack seemed heavy enough to push him through the asphalt pavement. And all about him was the faint jingle of equipment and the tramp of feet. Every part of him was full of sweat. He could feel vaguely the steam of sweat that rose from the ranks of struggling bodies about him. But gradually he forgot everything but the pack tugging at his shoulders, weighing down his thighs and ankles and feet, and the monotonous rhythm of his feet striking the pavement and of the other feet, in front of him, behind him, beside him, crunching, crunching.

From Three Soldiers *by John Dos Passos. Copyright © 1921, renewal of copyright 1949. Reprinted by permission of Mrs. John Dos Passos.*

Critical Thinking

1. Why, do you think, did the soldiers cheer when they were told that they were going overseas?
2. Where did Fuselli get most of his ideas for imagining the war in Europe?
3. What was Fuselli's attitude toward being in the army? Do you think this was typical of World War I soldiers?

Connecting History and Literature

Answer one question with a brief essay.

A. When and why did the United States join World War I?
B. What mood is created by the final paragraph of the excerpt?

Name _____   Date _____

WORKSHEET 26
Bartolomeo Vanzetti's Speech to the Jury

Nicola Sacco and Bartolomeo Vanzetti were convicted of murder and robbery in Massachusetts in 1920 and later executed. Below are excerpts from Vanzetti's last statement to the jury.

We have proved that there could not have been another Judge on the face of the earth more prejudiced and more cruel than you have been against us. We have proved that. Still they refuse the new trial. We know, and you know in your heart, that you have been against us from the very beginning, before you see us. Before you see us you already know that we were radicals, that we were underdogs, that we were the enemy of the institution that you can believe in good faith in their goodness. . . .

We know that you have spoke yourself and have spoke your hostility against us, and your despisement against us with friends of yours in the train, at the University Club of Boston, on the Golf Club of Worcester, Massachusetts. I am sure that if the people who know all what you say against us would have the civil courage to take the stand, maybe your Honor—I am sorry to say this because you are an old man, and I have an old father—but maybe you would be beside us in good justice at this time. . . .

We were tried during a time that has now passed into history. I mean by that, a time when there was hysteria of resentment and hate against the people of our principles, against the foreigner, against slackers, and it seems to me—rather, I am positive, that both you and Mr. Katzmann has done all what it were in your power in order to work out, in order to agitate still more the passion of the juror, the prejudice of the juror, against us. . . .

Well, I have already say that I not only am not guilty of these crimes, but I never commit a crime in my life,—I have never steal and I have never kill and I have never spilt blood, and I have fought against the crime, and I have fought and I have sacrificed myself even to eliminate the crimes that the law and the church legitimate and sanctify.

This is what I say: I would not wish to a dog or to a snake, to the most low and misfortunate creature on the earth—I would not wish to any of them what I have had to suffer for things that I am not guilty of. But my conviction is that I have suffered for things that I am guilty of. I am suffering for things that I am guilty of. I am suffering because I am a radical, and indeed I am a radical; I have suffered because I was an Italian, and indeed I am an Italian; I have suffered more for my family and for my beloved than for myself; but I am so convinced to be right that if you could execute me two times, and if I could be reborn two other times, I would live again to do what I have done already. I have finished. Thank you.

Quoted in The Sacco-Vanzetti Case, *by Osmond K. Fraenkel (Alfred Knopf, 1931).*

Comprehension

1. Did Vanzetti believe that Judge Thayer had been fair and impartial? Give evidence to support your answer.
2. Vanzetti said he had suffered for his guilt. What "crimes" did he mention?

Critical Thinking

3. Some people likened the execution of Sacco and Vanzetti to the executions during the Salem Witchcraft Trials in the 1600s. Do you agree with this comparison? Explain your reasons.

WORSHEET 26
F. Scott Fitzgerald, *The Great Gatsby*

Literature

F. Scott Fitzgerald's stories of "the rich and famous" of the Jazz Age did more than describe the era—they helped create its ideal lifestyle. Fitzgerald's novel *The Great Gatsby* (1925) tells the story of a millionaire with a mysterious past. In this scene, Nick Carraway (the book's narrator) and Daisy Buchanan visit Jay Gatsby's Long Island mansion.

"My house looks well, doesn't it?" he [Gatsby] demanded. "See how the whole front of it catches the light."

I agreed that it was splendid.

"Yes." His eyes went over it, every arched door and square tower. "It took me just three years to earn the money that bought it."

"I thought you inherited your money."

"I did, old sport," he said automatically, "but I lost most of it in the big panic—the panic of the war."

I think he hardly knew what he was saying, for when I asked him what business he was in he answered "That's my affair," before he realized that it wasn't an appropriate reply.

"Oh, I've been in several things," he corrected himself. "I was in the drug business and then I was in the oil business. But I'm not in either one now." He looked at me with more attention. "Do you mean you've been thinking over what I proposed the other night?"

Before I could answer, Daisy came out of the house and two rows of brass buttons on her dress gleamed in the sunlight.

"That huge place *there*?" she cried pointing.

"Do you like it?"

"I love it, but I don't see how you live there all alone."

"I keep it always full of interesting people, night and day. People who do interesting things. Celebrated people." . . .

We went upstairs, through period bedrooms swathed in rose and lavender silk and vivid with new flowers, through dressing-rooms and poolrooms, and bathrooms with sunken baths—intruding into one chamber where a dishevelled man in pajamas was doing liver exercises on the floor. It was Mr. Klipspringer, the "boarder." I had seen him wandering hungrily about the beach that morning. Finally we came to Gatsby's own apartment, a bedroom and a bath and an Adam study, where we sat down and drank a glass of some Chartreuse he took from a cupboard in the wall.

He hadn't once ceased looking at Daisy and I think he revalued everything in his house according to the measure of response it drew from her well-loved eyes. Sometimes, too, he stared around at his possessions in a dazed way as though in her actual and astounding presence none of it was any longer real. Once he nearly toppled down a flight of stairs.

His bedroom was the simplest room of all—except where the dresser was garnished with a toilet set [comb, brush, mirror] of pure dull gold. Daisy took the brush with delight and smoothed her hair, whereupon Gatsby sat down and shaded his eyes and began to laugh.

"It's the funniest thing, old sport," he said hilariously. "I can't—when I try to—"

He had passed visibly through two states and was entering upon a third. After his embarrassment and his unreasoning joy he was consumed with wonder at her presence. He had been full of the idea so long, dreamed it right through to the end, waited with his teeth set, so to speak, at an inconceivable pitch of intensity. Now, in the reaction, he was running down like an overwound clock. . . .

After the house we were to see the grounds and the swimming pool and the hydroplane and the midsummer flowers—but outside Gatsby's window it began to rain again so we stood in a row looking at the corrugated surface of the Sound.

"If it wasn't for the mist we could see your home across the bay," said Gatsby. "You always have a green light that burns all night at the end of your dock."

Daisy put her arm through his abruptly but he seemed absorbed in what he had just said. Possibly it had occurred to him that the colossal significance of that light had now vanished forever. Compared to the great distance that had separated him from Daisy it

had seemed very near to her, almost touching her. It had seemed as close as a star to the moon. Now it was again a green light on a dock. His count of enchanted objects had diminished by one.

From The Great Gatsby *(Authorized Text) by F. Scott Fitzgerald. Copyright 1925 by Charles Scribner's Sons; renewal copyright 1953 by Frances Scott Fitzgerald Lanahan. Copyright © 1991, 1992 by Eleanor Lanahan, Matthew Bruccoli, and Samuel J. Lanahan as Trustees u/a dated 7/3/75, created by Frances Scott Fitzgerald Smith.*

Critical Thinking

1. According to what Gatsby says here, how did historical events affect the ups and downs of his fortune?
2. Were Nick and Daisy impressed with Gatsby's wealth? Explain.
3. How does Gatsby's behavior show that he was not yet completely used to being rich?

Connecting History and Literature

Answer one question with a brief essay.

A. How does Gatsby's way of life reflect the prosperity of the 1920s?
B. What does Gatsby love most? What might be Fitzgerald's message?

WORKSHEET 27   **Primary Source**
Living Through the Depression

Americans suffered for more than ten years through the Great Depression that followed the stock market crash of 1929. At the height of the Depression in 1933, about 13 million Americans were out of work, and many others had only part-time jobs. The excerpt below describes the effect of joblessness on some of the people who lived through the Depression.

In every American city, quantities of families were being evicted from their inadequate apartments; moving in with other families till ten or twelve people would be sharing three or four rooms; or shivering through the winter in heatless houses because they could afford no coal, eating meat once a week or not at all. If employers sometimes found that former employees who had been discharged did not seem eager for re-employment ("They won't take a job if you offer them one!"), often the reason was panic: a dreadful fear of inadequacy which was one of the Depression's commonest psychopathological results. A woman clerk, offered piecework after being jobless for a year, confessed that she almost had not dared to come to the office, she had been in such terror lest she wouldn't know where to hang her coat, wouldn't know how to find the washroom, wouldn't understand the boss's directions for her job.

For perhaps the worst thing about this Depression was its inexorable continuance year after year. Men who have been sturdy and self-respecting workers can take unemployment without flinching for a few weeks, a few months, even if they have to see their families suffer; but it is different after a year . . . two years . . . three years. . . . Among the miserable creatures curled up on park benches or standing in dreary lines before the soup kitchens in 1932 were men who had been jobless since the end of 1929.

From Since Yesterday: The Nineteen-Thirties in America *by Frederick Lewis Allen. Copyright 1939, 1940 by Frederick Lewis Allen, renewed copyright © 1968 by Agnes Rodgers Allen. Published by Harper & Row, Publishers, Inc.*

Comprehension

1. How were American families affected by the Depression, according to the author?
2. According to the author, how did long-term unemployment affect workers' ability to apply for jobs?

Critical Thinking

3. What does the author suggest was the worst thing about the Depression?
4. From what sources could the homeless and unemployed find help under the Hoover administration? Use your textbook as needed to answer this question.

WORSHEET 27 ~~WORSHEET~~

WORKSHEET 27   **Literature**
John P. Marquand, *Point of No Return*

The stock market crash of 1929 was one of those milestone events that people remembered long afterward—where they were when they heard the news, how the events affected them and the people around them. Many writers of the 1930s and 1940s used the stock market crash as a turning point in their novels and short stories. This excerpt from John P. Marquand's 1949 novel *Point of No Return* describes the events in the life of Charles Gray at the time of the stock market crash.

During all of his [Charles's] later business experience, many otherwise reasonable people kept resurrecting the details of the crash of 1929. They discussed it, apparently, for the same reason that old ladies enjoyed describing surgical operations and sessions with their dentists. There was a snob value in boasting of old pain. Instead of wishing to forget, they kept struggling to remember: The older men would talk about Black Friday in the nineties [1890s] and the more technical panic of 1907 as though all these debacles were just alike. . . . There were even people, who should have known better, who seemed to be imbued [filled] with the fixed idea that the crash of 1929 caused the depression. They could no longer see it as a symptom or as an extreme example of mass hysteria. Only unattractively strong individuals should have been allowed to dabble in that market.

Most people never seemed to see what Charles saw in the crash—a sordidly [dirtily] ugly exhibition of the basest [most evil] of human fears. They had forgotten the desperation that made cowards and thieves out of previously respectable people, and the fear evolved from greed which had no decency or dignity. Instead, they always harked back to the spectacular—the confusion, the lights in downtown New York burning night after night while clerks were struggling to balance the brokerage accounts; and sooner or later they always asked Charles where he had been working then and whether he too had been long on the market on that particular day in October. He had learned long ago to answer accurately, with only part of the truth. He always said that he had been in Boston with E. P. Rush & Company and nothing much had happened to him. He had made some money out of the market the year before and had put it into government bonds. . . .

He never told the whole truth to anyone, except to Nancy and to Arthur Slade, and Arthur Slade may have told some of it to Tony Burton at the Stuyvesant Bank but Charles was never sure. . . . There were some things which were better not told, and there was no use digging up what was so completely finished. His own illusions and everything he had planned had crashed in that common crash, but then millions of lives and plans had been crashing ever since. It did no good to imagine what he might have done to have prevented it. Actually he could have done nothing. Everything was what Mr. Lovell would have called an accomplished fact before Charles had been permitted to face it. He was always glad he did not have to blame himself, at least not very much.

When the drop occurred in September, that minor break which nearly everyone considered a normal readjustment considering the market's phenomenally unbroken rise, he had seen it for what it was—the first rumblings of a landslide, an ominous shift of stress and strain that would never strike a balance until the whole structure broke. He knew this was the beginning of a greater break even before Mr. Rush, after a partners' meeting, called him in to help compose a letter advising customers of Rush & Company to sell their holdings of common stocks. . . .

The day when the market first broke in

October must have started for everyone the way it did for Charles, as a part of the ordinary routine of living. He remembered reading later, in a brochure published by a banking house: "In years to come the 1929 crash will doubtless be remembered merely as a summer thundershower." When this was written prosperity was still just around the corner and happy days like those old happy ones would be here again if you were not a bear on the United States. When the storm did break, in a cloudless sky, work went on that first day without much interruption in conservative offices like Rush & Company. It was only when the drop went on the next day and the next and when the tickers lagged further and further behind the trading that Charles began to observe that all the faces in the office were stamped with an expression that began to erase individuality.

Jessica had come to Boston on the morning of the break and they were to have had lunch together but he had called her up at her aunt's house to say that, although it had nothing to do with his own department, he felt he had better stay at the office on general principles. Yet at home for the first day or so he could not notice any change and there seemed to be no more connection between home and E. P. Rush & Company than there ever had been. Back in Clyde [a fictional Boston suburb] he could forget the crowd around the board and those sickly individual attempts at indifference and composure [self-control].

That first evening before supper, his father said it would be nice if Axel were to mix some Martini cocktails because it had been quite a day in Boston and Dorothea and Elbridge were coming to dinner. Elbridge had something particular to tell them and he hoped that Elbridge had not been monkeying with the market. It was impossible to read anything on his father's face but as soon as they had a moment alone together Charles asked him if everything was all right, and his father looked very cheerful.

"I wish you wouldn't try to look like a doctor," he said, "and I wish you wouldn't think of me as a widow or an orphan. Hasn't everybody been expecting this? Of course I'm all right."

He was like all the rest of them. They were already beginning to say that they had seen it coming, but Charles felt deeply relieved. His father drank two Martinis, which was unusual for him, but he did not speak again about the market.

From Point of No Return by *John P. Marquand. Copyright © 1947, 1948, 1949 by John P. Marquand. By permission of Little, Brown and Company.*

Critical Thinking

1. To what earlier economic problems did the older men compare the stock market crash of 1929?
2. What current events does the author incorporate into this section of the novel?
3. What does Charles see as the cause of the stock market crash?

Connecting History and Literature

Answer one question with a brief essay.

A. Did the Crash of 1929 "cause" the Depression or merely "trigger" it? Explain.
B. How can changes in the public's mood affect the economy?

WORKSHEET 28
The Black Experience

Primary Source

Richard Wright was born in Mississippi in 1908. His first novel, *Native Son,* published in 1940, brought him immediate fame. A year later he published *12 Million Black Voices,* which vividly portrays the life of blacks in America. Following are excerpts from that book.

We are children of the black sharecroppers, the first-born of the city tenements.

We have tramped down a road three hundred years long. We have been shunted to and fro by cataclysmic social changes.

We are a fold born of cultural devastation, slavery, physical suffering, unrequited longing, abrupt emancipation, migration, disillusionment, bewilderment, joblessness, and insecurity—all enacted within a *short* space of historical time! . . .

There are some of us who feel our hurts so deeply that we find it impossible to work with whites; we feel that it is futile to hope or dream in terms of American life. Our distrust is so great that we form intensely racial and nationalistic organizations and advocate the establishment of a separate state, a forty-ninth state, in which we black folk would live. . . .

In 1929, when millions of us black folk were jobless, many unemployed white workers joined with us on a national scale to urge relief measures and adequate housing. The influence of this united effort spread even into the South where black and white sharecroppers were caught in the throes of futile conflict. . . .

Not all black folk, however, reacted to the depression in this manner. There were hundreds of thousands of us who saw that we bought our groceries from white clerks, . . . that we paid our rent to white realtors, . . . that we asked jobs of white bosses. . . ; in short, that we had no word to say about anything that happened in our lives. . . .

We black folk, our history and our present being, are a mirror of all the manifold experiences of America. What we want, what we represent, what we endure is what America *is.* If we black folk perish, America will perish. . . .

The differences between black folk and white folk are not blood or color, and the ties that bind us are deeper than those that separate us. The common road of hope which we all have traveled has brought us into a stronger kinship than any words, laws, or legal claims.

Look at us and know us and you will know yourselves, for *we* are *you,* looking back at you from the dark mirror of our lives!

What do black folk want?

We want what others have, the right to share in the upward march of American life, the only life we remember or have ever known. . . .

From 12 Million Voices *by Richard Wright. Copyright © 1941 by Richard Wright, Copyright © 1969 by Arno Press, Inc.*

Comprehension

1. What types of suffering have blacks endured? (See the third paragraph.)
2. What experiences did blacks have working with whites during the Depression?

Critical Thinking

3. What does Wright feel is necessary in order for America to survive?

WORKSHEET 28
Paul Yee, "'Ginger for the Heart"

Literature

In 1848 gold was discovered in northern California. This discovery start-ed a world gold rush. People from the East Coast of the United States as well as from other countries traveled thousands of miles to reach Califor-nia and try their luck at gold mining. Chinese immigrants poured into California at this time. Many were hired as laborers to help construct the new transcontinental railroad, but others headed for the mountain streams of the Sierra Nevadas, where they panned for gold dust and nuggets that were mired with the sand in the bottom of the streams. The story below comes from Paul Yee's collection of fictional stories about Chi-nese immigrants living in the United States.

The buildings of Chinatown are stoutly con-structed of brick, and while some are broad and others thin, they rise no higher than four solid storeys. Many contain stained-glass windows decorated with flower and diamond patterns, and others boast bal-conies with fancy wrought-iron railings.

Only one building stands above the rest. Its turret-like tower is visible even from the harbor, because the cone-shaped roof is made of copper.

In the early days, Chang the merchant tailor owned this building. He used the main floor for his store and rented out the others. But he kept the tower room for his own use, for the sun filled it with light. This was the room where his wife and daughter worked.

His daughter's name was Yenna, and her beauty was beyond compare. She had ivory skin, sparkling eyes, and her hair hung long and silken, shining like polished ebony. All day long she and her mother sat by the tower window and sewed with silver needles and silken threads. They sang songs while they worked, and their voices rose in wondrous harmonies.

In all Chinatown, the craftsmanship of Yenna and her mother was considered the finest. Search as they might, customers could not discern [detect] where holes had once pierced their shirts. Buttonholes never stretched out of shape, and seams were all but invisible.

One day, a young man came into the store laden with garments for mending. His shoul-ders were broad and strong, yet his eyes were soft and caring. Many times he came, and many times he saw Yenna. For hours he would sit and watch her work. They fell deeply in love, though few words were spo-ken between them.

Spring came and boats bound for the northern gold fields began to sail again. It was time for the young man to go. He had borrowed money to pay his way over to the New World, and now he had to repay his debts. Onto his back he threw his blankets and tools, food and warm jackets. Then he set off with miners from around the world, clutching gold pans and shovels.

Yenna had little to give him in farewell. All she found in the kitchen was a ginger root as large as her hand. As she stroked its brown knobs and bumpy eyes, she whispered to him, "This will warm you in the cold weather. I will wait for you, but, like this piece of ginger, I, too, will age and grow dry." Then she pressed her lips to the ginger, and turned away.

"I will come back," the young man said. "The fire burning for you in my heart can never be extinguished."

Thereafter, Yenna lit a lamp at every nightfall and set it in the tower window. Rains lashed against the glass, snow piled low along the ledge, and ocean winds rattled the frame. But the flame did not waver, even though the young man never sent letters. Yenna did not weep uselessly, but continued to sew and sing with her mother.

There were few unmarried women in Chinatown, and many men came to seek Yenna's hand in marriage. Rich gold miners and sons of successful merchants bowed before her, but she always looked away. They gave her grand gifts, but still she shook her head, until finally the men grew weary and called her crazy. In China, parents arranged all marriages, and daughters became the property of their husbands. But Chang the merchant tailor treasured his daughter's happiness and let her be.

One winter, an epidemic ravaged the city. When it was over, Chang had lost his wife and his eyesight. Yenna led him up to the tower where he could feel the sun and drifting clouds move across his face. She began to sew again, and while she sewed, she sang for her father. The lamp continued to burn steadily at the tower window as she worked. With twice the amount of work to do, she labored long after dusk. She fed the flame more oil and sent her needle skimming through the heavy fabrics. Nimbly her fingers braided shiny cords and coiled them into butterfly buttons. And when the wick sputtered into light each evening, Yenna's heart soared momentarily into her love's memories. Nights passed into weeks, months turned into years, and four years quickly flew by.

One day a dusty traveler came into the store and flung a bundle of ragged clothes onto the counter. Yenna shook out the first shirt, and out rolled a ginger root. Taking it into her hand, she saw that pieces had been nibbled off, but the core of the root was still firm and fragrant.

She looked up. There stood the man she had promised to wait for. His eyes appeared older and wiser.

"Your gift saved my life several times," he said. "The fire of the ginger is powerful indeed."

"Why is the ginger root still firm and heavy?" she wondered. "Should it not have dried and withered?"

"I kept it close to my heart and my sweat coated it. In lonely moments, my tears soaked it." His calloused hands reached out for her. "Your face has not changed."

"Nor has my heart," she replied. "I have kept a lamp burning all these years."

"So I have heard," he smiled. "Will you come away with me now? It has taken many years to gather enough gold to buy a farm. I have built you a house on my land."

For the first time since his departure, tears cascaded down Yenna's face. She shook her head. "I cannot leave. My father needs me."

"Please come with me," the young man pleaded. "You will be very happy, I promise."

Yenna swept the wetness from her cheeks. "Stay with me and work this store instead," she implored.

The young man stiffened and stated proudly, "A man does not live in his wife's house." And the eyes that she remembered so well gleamed with determination.

"But this is a new land," she cried. "Must we forever follow the old ways?"

She reached out for him, but he brushed her away. With a curse, he hurled the ginger root into the fireplace. As the flames leapt up, Yenna's eyes blurred. The young man clenched and unclenched his fists in anger. They stood like stone.

At last the man turned to leave, but suddenly he knelt at the fireplace. Yenna saw him reach in with the tongs and pull something out of the flames.

"Look!" he whispered in amazement. "The ginger refuses to be burnt! The flames cannot touch it!"

Yenna looked and saw black burn marks charring the root, but when she took it in her hand, she found it still firm and moist. She held it to her nose, and found the fragrant sharpness still there.

The couple embraced and swore to stay together. They were married at a lavish banquet attended by all of Chinatown. There, the father passed his fingers over his son-in-law's face and nodded in satisfaction.

Shortly after, the merchant Chang died, and the young couple moved away. Yenna sold the business and locked up the tower room. But on nights when boats pull in from far away, they say a flicker of light can still be seen in that high window. And Chinese women are reminded that ginger is one of their best friends.

Critical Thinking

1. Why did Yenna light a lamp every night and place it in the tower window?
2. Why did Yenna and the young man argue after his return?
3. What lesson did Yenna and the young man learn from the ginger root's refusal to burn?

Reprinted by permission of Macmillan Books for Young Readers, an imprint of Simon & Schuster Children's Publishing Division from Tales from Gold Mountain *by Paul Yee. Copyright © 1989 Paul Yee.*

Connecting History and Literature

Answer one question with a brief essay.

A. How is the conflict near the end of this story symbolic of the feelings of many immigrants?
B. Is "Ginger for the Heart" a Chinese story, an American story, or both? Explain.

Name _____   Date _____

WORKSHEET 29
Ernie Pyle, War Correspondent

Ernie Pyle was probably the most famous correspondent of World War II.
He wrote about the war from the point of view of the average soldier in
the trenches. The passage below is from an article written by Pyle on
June 7, 1944, the day after D-Day.

I took a walk along the historic coast of Normandy in the country of France. It was a lovely day for strolling along the seashore. Men were sleeping on the sand, some of them sleeping forever. Men were floating in the water, but they didn't know they were in the water, for they were dead.

The water was full of squishy little jelly-fish about the size of a man's hand. Millions of them. In the center of each of them was a green design exactly like a four-leafed clover. The good-luck emblem. Sure. . . .

I walked for a mile and a half along the water's edge of our many-miled invasion beach. I walked slowly, for the detail on that beach was infinite.

The wreckage was vast and startling. The awful waste and destruction of war, even aside from the loss of human life, has always been one of its outstanding features to those who are in it. Anything and everything is expendable. and we did expend on our beachhead in Normandy during those first few hours.

For a mile out from the beach there were scores of tanks and trucks and boats that were not visible, for they were at the bottom of the water—swamped by overloading, or hit by shells, or sunk by mines. Most of their crews were lost.

There were trucks tipped half over and swamped, partly sunken barges, and the angled-up corners of jeeps, and small land-ing craft half submerged. And at low tide you could still see those vicious six-pronged iron snares that helped snag and wreck them.

On the beach itself, high and dry, were all kinds of wrecked vehicles. There were tanks that had only just made the beach before being knocked out. There were jeeps that had burned to a dull gray. There were big derricks on caterpillar treads that didn't quite make it. There were half-tracks carrying office equipment that had been made into a shambles by a single shell hit, their interiors still holding the useless equipage of smashed typewriters, telephones, office files. . . .

On the beach lay, expended, sufficient men and mechanism for a small war. They were gone forever now. And yet we could afford it.

We could afford it because we were on, we had our toe hold, and behind us there were such enormous replacements for this wreckage on the beach that you could hardly conceive of the sum total. Men and equipment were flowing from England in such a gigantic stream that it made the waste on the beachhead seem like nothing at all, really nothing at all.

From Brave Men *by Ernie Pyle. Copyright © 1943, 1944 by Scripps-Howard Newspaper Alliance. Copyright 1944 by Henry Holt and Co. Copyright ©1971, 1972 by Holt, Rinehart and Winston.*

Comprehension

1. What did Pyle say was one of the outstanding features of war?
2. Why did Pyle say that the waste on the beachhead seemed "like nothing at all"?

Critical Thinking

3. Pyle created a powerful picture of the beachhead at Normandy by combining facts, opinions, and values. Which fact do you find most powerful?

WORSHEET 29

Literature

John Hersey, *The Wall*

World War II inspired powerful literature. John Hersey wrote several novels showing the impact of war on civilians in Europe and Asia. *The Wall* is written as the fictional journal of Noach (NO-ahk) Levinson. This excerpt discusses the efforts of Jews of Poland's Warsaw Ghetto to resist the German occupiers.

EVENTS SEPTEMBER 5–12, 1942. ENTRY SEPTEMBER 14, 1942. N. L. [Noach Levinson] We are calling this horrible experience "the Kettle." The Germans' purpose seems to have been to disrupt our order completely—moving us from our homes, invalidating our previous system of working cards, and thereby shaking out all those who had managed before those days improperly to evade deportation. They shut us up in a manageable area—the "Kettle"—and combed through our helpless crowd. According to the best estimate I can make, we numbered about 120,000 when the "Kettle" was put on the stove, so to speak. The German figures on deportation for the six days are 47,791 Jews taken. On one day, September 8, they took 13,596—the worst day we have had. It may be that this was the worst day in all of Jewish history—up to now, at any rate. There are today perhaps 70,000 of us left here in the ghetto, where once half a million Jews were crowded together.

Our first warning of the "Kettle" came when the Germans put up posters. . . .

EVENTS SEPTEMBER 4, 1942. ENTRY DITTO. N. L. Berson and I were walking in the streets together when we saw the first poster.

N. L., after I had read only a few words: "The noose is tightening."

The poster commanded that by ten o'clock tomorrow morning all Jews remaining within the Large Ghetto are to gather for registration purposes. . . . They are directed to bring food for two days and drinking utensils, and to leave their apartments unlocked. Anyone found outside the designated area six city blocks by two, to contain more than a hundred thousand Jews, will be shot.

Berson, with earnest expression: "Soon we must choose: either die fighting or die like sheep in a shambles." I think he is right, but how could we ever make such a choice?

EVENTS SEPTEMBER 5–10, 1942. ENTRY SEPTEMBER 11, 1942. FROM DOLEK BERSON. . . . For a time Berson and Rachel let themselves be pushed and carried by the crowd now half a block toward Zamenhofa Street, now back a few yards toward Lubetzkiego, purposelessly. At the sound of a shot down the street to the eastward, part of the mob recoiled and with a violent surge broke through into Ostrowska Street, which was itself crowded, and there the meaningless undulations began again. Nothing seemed to be happening. Berson and Rachel exchanged only brief mutterings. Berson says he was impatient with Rachel. He felt as if he were in the grip of a bad dream; he had the sensation of struggling to wake up and being unable to. The crowd pushed and pulled.

It was late afternoon before Berson recovered from his dazed, dreamlike state. Suddenly once he looked down and saw and felt Rachel beating on his chest with her fists, crying: "Do something! Do something!" They came to a place where the mob was, if possible, thicker than elsewhere. Berson lifted Rachel up above the heads of the people to see what she could see. She told him that a huge selection was taking place at the street corner. Berson eased her down and said: "Why should we go to them? Let them come and get us!"

Most of the houses and courtyards were barricaded or guarded, but Berson and Rachel found one into which the mob had broken, and they went inside and climbed a staircase and with many others jumped from a second-story window into the next court-yard and broke through a fence behind that into still another and climbed high in a building and got out onto some roofs (by this time the sky was darkening) and crossed the roofs until they found a skylight, which they broke (now there were fewer people, perhaps a score; the group bad scattered on the roofs) and they let themselves down into an empty apartment house and went into one of them and threw themselves on the beds and lay there through the night, hearing shots and screams all night near by and naturally not sleeping, and stayed there half the next day until curiosity and fear made them go out and down the stairs of the apartment to the street level, but when they saw, in the court-yard, a pile of perhaps thirty bloody Jewish corpses, newly executed, they drew back and climbed again into the same apartment, this time taking the precaution, however, of observing and preparing three different escape routes downstairs into some cellars and out an areaway; up through the sky-light; and, as a third choice, out into the courtyard past the corpses and directly into the street—and during the second night they had occasion to be thankful for this fore-sight, because at a late hour they heard foot-steps and the shouts of German hunters, and escaping by the skylight, they spent the hot night shivering on the roofs, listening to shots and screams below, and in the soft dawn they returned yet once more to the same apartment, on the theory that the chances of its being searched again immedi-ately were slight. . . .

And thus, in what seemed a scarcely punc-tuated continuity of terror, movement, vigi-lance, hunger, filth, and bare survival, returning again and again to the same apartment, Berson and Rachel passed six days without facing the peripatetic selec-tions. At the end of six days it was over. A few of the former tenants of the apartment came home and said it was over. The Ger-mans . . . had left the "registration area." Berson and Rachel went through hushed and dreary streets to Pavel's shop.

From The Wall *by John Hersey. Copyright 1950 by John Hersey. Reprinted by permission of Alfred A. Knopf Inc.*

Critical Thinking

1. Describe the different reactions of Jews in the Warsaw Ghetto to German efforts to destroy them.
2. What do the first few sentences tell you about the restrictions imposed on Jews in the ghetto even before the Nazis stepped up the persecutions?
3. What does Berson conclude is the real aim of the "registration" order?

Connecting History and Literature

Answer one question with a brief essay.

A. When and how had Poland come under German control?
B. How are the events described in this excerpt related to the Holocaust?

WORSHEET 30
Letters from a Soldier in Vietnam

First Lieutenant James Simmen served as an infantry platoon leader south of Saigon during 1968. The following excerpts are from letters he wrote to his brother while in Vietnam.

13 March [1968]

Hi Vern,

. . . A friend got killed on an ambush last week. [The colonel] told him to move in the middle of the night. As he drew in all his claymores [mines], Charlie [the enemy] hit. Last night they told me to move twice. It'll be a cold day . . . when I move. Thirty minutes later I reported "Moved." The colonel isn't about to come out to see where I am. I'm chicken but not stupid! . . .

Hi Vern,

Get your letters today. It was great hearing from you. Actually, I can't summarize my feelings of my trip to Australia [for rest and relaxation]. I don't know if I had a fabulous time or not. It was weird. Getting back to a completely English-looking and -speaking country made me feel kind of ashamed of the way I've thought and acted over here. I realize that I've actually enjoyed some of the things I've done which would be repulsive to a healthy mind. This place does make you sick in the head. . . .

Hello Vern,

. . . I got your letter dated 4 July asking about ambushes and booby traps. . . . I'd always have civilians walk point for me. They ranged from 14-year-olds to men with canes, but they never hit a booby trap whereas all the other platoons [got] men hurt and killed. . . .

I'm becoming quite conservative in my ideas and tastes here. When you see men suffer and die for principles, and take it so great, it's hard to forgive the liberals and free thinkers crying over nothing.

Your brother,
Jim

Letter excerpt by 1Lt. James Simmen, platoon leader with the 5th Battalion, 60th Infantry (Mechanized), 9th Infantry Division in the area south of Saigon during 1968. From Dear America: Letters Home From Vietnam, *Edited by Bernard Edelman. Copyright 1985 by The New York Vietnam Veterans Memorial Commission.*

Comprehension

1. How did James Simmen mislead his colonel? Why did he do it?
2. What awareness did Simmen have as a result of his vacation to Australia?
3. To *walk point* means to walk some distance ahead of a patrol. Why would having civilians walk point help save his men?

Critical Thinking

4. Simmen expressed his resentment of "liberals and free thinkers crying over nothing." Why might some American soldiers in Vietnam have felt this way?

WORKSHEET 30
Oscar Hijuelos, *The Mambo Kings Play Songs of Love*

The revolution in Cuba led by Fidel Castro brought a wide range of reactions in the United States, especially among Cuban Americans. Oscar Hijuelo's novel *The Mambo Kings Play Songs of Love* tells the story of the brothers Nestor and Cesar Castillo, Cuban musicians—the Mambo Kings—who have been in New York since 1949. The high point of their memories is an appearance on the "I Love Lucy" show. Here is how the turmoil in Cuba affected Cesar Castillo.

Of course, it was a pleasure to perform for the people again. Got his mind off things. And it always made him happy when someone would come along and ask him for an autograph (*"Ciertamente!"*). It felt good when he'd go walking along the 125th Street markets on a Sunday afternoon and some guy in a sleeveless T-shirt would call out to him from a window, "Hey! Mambo King, how's it going?"

Still he felt his sadness. Sometimes when he played those jobs with Manny, he would get a ride back home. But most often he rode the subways, as he didn't like to drive at night anymore. . . .

Anonymous in a pair of sunglasses and with his hat pulled low over his brow, guitar or trumpet case wedged between his knees, the Mambo King traveled to his jobs around the city. It was easy to get home when he worked restaurants in the Village or Madison Avenue bars, where he would serenade the Fred MacMurray-looking executives and their companions ("Now, girls, sing after me, Babalooooooo!"), as those jobs usually ended around eleven at night. But when he'd play small clubs and dance halls out on the edges of Brooklyn and the Bronx, he'd get home at four-thirty, five in the morning. Spending many a night riding the trains by himself, he'd read *La Prensa* or *El Diario* [Spanish-language newspapers] or the *Daily News*.

He made lots of friends on the trains; he knew the flamenco guitarist from Toledo, Spain, a fellow named Eloy Garcia, who played in the Café Madrid; an accordionist with a tango orchestra in Greenwich Village, named Macedonio, a roly-poly fellow who'd go to work in a gaucho hat. . . . He knew Estela and Nilda, two *zarzuela* singers who would pass through matronhood with wilting carnations in their hair. He knew a black three-man dance team with conk hairdos, friendly and hopeful fellows, resplendent in white tuxedos and spats, who were always heading out to do auditions. ("These days we're hoping to get on the Ed Sullivan show.") Then there were the Mexicans with their over-sized guitars, trumpets, and an accordion that resembled an altar, its fingerboard shiny with hammer-flattened religious medals. . . . The men wore big sombreros and trousers that jangled with bells, and high, thinheeled cowboy boots, leather-etched with swirly flowers, and traveled with a woman and a little girl. The woman wore a mantilla and a frilly dress made of Aztec-looking fabric; the little girl wore a red dress and played a tambourine on which an enamel likeness of John the Baptist had been painted. She'd sit restlessly, unhappily during the rides, while Cesar would lean forward and speak quietly to her mother: ("How is it going with you today?" "Slow lately, the best time is during Christmas, and then everybody gives.") They'd ride to the last stop downtown, to the Staten Island Ferry terminal, where they would play *bambas, corridos, huapangos,* and *rancheras* for the waiting passengers.

"*Que Dios te bendiga*. God bless you."

"The same to you."

There were others, a lot of Latin musicians like himself on their way to weary late-night jobs in the deepest reaches of Brooklyn and the Bronx. Some were young and didn't know the name Cesar Castillo, but the old-timers, the musicians who had been kicking around in New York since the forties, they knew him. Trumpet players, guitarists, and drummers would come over and sit with the Mambo King.

Still there were the tunnels, the darkness, the dense solitude of a station at four in the morning, and the Mambo King daydreaming about Cuba.

It made a big difference to him that he just couldn't get on an airplane and fly down to Havana to see his daughter or to visit the family in Las Piñas.

Who would ever have dreamed that would be so? That Cuba would be chums with Russia?

It was all a new kind of sadness.

Sitting in his room in the Hotel Splendour . . . the Mambo King preferred not to think about the revolution in Cuba. What . . . had he ever cared about Cuban politics in the old days, except for when he might play a political rally in the provinces for some local crooked politician? What . . . had he cared when the consensus among his musician pals was that it wouldn't make any difference who came to power, until Fidel. What could he have done about it, anyway? Things must have been pretty bad. The orchestra leader Rene Touzet had fled to Miami with his sons, playing the big hotels there and concerts for the Cubans. Then came the grand master of Cuban music, Ernesto Lecuona, arriving in Miami distraught and in a state of creative torpor, unable to play a note on his piano and ending up in Puerto Rico, "bitter and disenchanted," before he died, he'd heard some people say. Bitter because his Cuba no longer existed.

God, all the Cubans were worked up. Even that *compañero*—who never forgot the family—Desi Arnaz had scribbled a little extra message on one of his Christmas cards: "We Cubans should stick together in these troubled times."

What had a friend called the revolution? "The rose that sprouted a thorn."

The great Celia Cruz would come to the States, too, in 1967. (On the other hand, Pala de Nieve—the musician "Snowball"—and the singer Elena Burke chose to remain behind.)

When his mother had died in 1962, the news came in a telegram from Eduardo [another brother still in Cuba], and a funny thing, too, because he had been thinking about her a lot that week, almost a soft pulsing in his heart, and his head filled with memories. And when he first read the line "I have bad news," he instantly thought "No." After reading the telegram, all he could do for hours was to . . . remember how she would take him into the yard as a child and wash his hair in a tub, again and again and again, her soft hands that smelled of rose water scrubbing his head and touching his face, the sun down through the treetops, her hair swirling with curls of light. . . .

The man cried for hours, until his eyelids were swollen, and he fell asleep with his head against the worktable.

Wished he had seen her one more time. Told himself that he would have gone back the previous year when he'd first heard that she had gotten sick, if it hadn't been for Castro.

Sometimes he got into big arguments with Ana Maria's husband, Raúl, about the situation down there. A long-time union man, Raúl kept himself busy organizing union shops in factories in the West Twenties, where most of the workers were immigrants from Central America and Puerto Rico. They were still friends, despite their differences of opinion. But Raúl kept trying to persuade the Mambo King about Castro. On a Friday night he went so far as to bring him down to a club on 14th Street where old Spanish and Portuguese leftists held meetings. He sat in the back listening as the old Spaniards, their expressions and politics shaped by beatings and jail terms in Franco's Spain, gave long, heartfelt speeches about "what must be done," which always came down to "*Viva el socialismo!*" and "Viva Fidel!"

Nothing wrong with doing away with the world's evils. He had seen a lot of that. In Cuba there had been rotting sheds made of cardboard and crates, skeleton children and dying dogs. A funeral procession in a small town called Minas. On the side of the plain pine coffin, a sign: *"Muerto de hambre."* ["Died of hunger."] On the street corners where the handsome *suavecitos* hung out talking, some guy who'd lost a limb while working at the sugar mill, in the *calderas*, begging. . . .

He had no argument with wanting to help others, Raúl. Back in Cuba, the people took care of their own. Families giving clothing, food, money, and, sometimes, a job in the household or in a business.

"My own mother, Raúl, listen to me. My own mother was always giving money to the poor, even when we didn't have very much. What more could anyone ask?"

"More."

"Raúl, you're my friend. I don't want to argue with you, but the people are leaving because they can't bear it."

From The Mambo Kings Play Songs of Love *by Oscar Hijuelos. Copyright ©1989 by Oscar Hijuelos. Reprinted by permission of Farrar Straus Giroux.*

Critical Thinking

1. What are some of the different cultures represented among the New Yorkers that Cesar knew?
2. How did the revolution in Cuba affect Cesar personally?
3. What was Raúl's opinion about the revolution? How did Cesar answer his arguments?
4. How did memories of the Spanish Civil War influence some of the older Spanish people?

Connecting History and Literature

Answer one question with a brief essay.

A. How did Cuba become a "battleground" of the cold war?
B. Explain why Cuban immigrants to the United States were among the most vocal opponents of Castro's government.

WORKSHEET 31
The Watergate Tapes, June 1972

Primary Source

When President Nixon was forced to give his tapes to the Senate committee investigating the Watergate scandal, they revealed that Nixon had approved a cover-up on June 23, 1972, just six days after the Watergate break-in. Below are transcripts from the June 23 tapes of a conversation between Nixon and Chief of Staff Bob Haldeman. (*H* is Haldeman and *P* is President Nixon.)

H: Now, on the investigation, you know the Democratic break-in thing, we're back in the problem area because the FBI is not under control, because [Pat] Gray [head of the FBI] doesn't exactly know how to control it and . . . their investigation is now leading into productive areas . . . and it goes in some directions we don't want it to go. . . .

P: That's right.

H: . . . The way to handle this now is for us to have Walters [Deputy Director of the CIA] call Pat Gray and just say, "Stay the . . . out of this—this is ah, business here we don't want you to go any further on it."

P: What about Pat Gray—you mean Pat Gray doesn't want to [drop the investigation]?

H: Pat does want to. He doesn't know how, and he doesn't have, he doesn't have any basis for doing it. Given this, he will then have the basis.

P: Yeah.

H: He'll . . . say, "We've got the signal from across the river to put the hold on this." And that will fit rather well because the FBI agents who are working the case, at this point, feet that's what it is.

P: This is CIA? They've traced the money [paid to the Watergate burglars]? Who'd they trace it to?

H: Ken Dahlberg.

P: Who is . . . Ken Dahlberg?

H: He gave $25,000 in Minnesota [to Nixon's re-election committee] and, ah, the check went directly to this guy Barker [one of the burglars].

P: It isn't from the [re-election] Committee though . . . ?

H: Yeah. It is. It's directly traceable and there's some more through some Texas people that went to the Mexican bank which can also be traced to the Mexican bank—they'll get their names today.

P: . . . I'm just thinking if they don't cooperate [with the investigation], what do they say? That they were approached by the Cubans. That's what Dahlberg has to say, the Texans too, that they—

H: Well, if they will. But then we're relying on more and more people all the time. That's the problem and they'll stop if we could take this other route [through the CIA].

P: All right.

Quoted in The Last Nixon Watch, *by John Osborne (The New Republic Book Company, Inc., 1975).*

Comprehension

1. What two specific problems did Haldeman point out to President Nixon?
2. What plan did they come up with to solve the problem?
3. Who was involved in the Watergate cover-up, according to this tape?

Critical Thinking

4. What charges were brought against President Nixon by the Senate committee investigating the Watergate break-in? Use your textbook as needed to answer this question.
5. What did this scandal reveal about the strength of the Constitution of the United States?

WORSHEET 31
Lillian Hellman, *Scoundrel Time*

Literature

Senator McCarthy and the House Un-American Activities Committee (HUAC) targeted many writers and filmmakers in their investigations. One was playwright Lillian Hellman, who testifed before HUAC in 1952. Hellman told the committee that she would testify only about her own actions and refused to answer questions about other people, as many so-called "friendly witnesses" were doing. Although Hellman was one of the country's leading dramatists, she was blacklisted from screenwriting. Later, she wrote *Scoundrel Time,* an account of her experiences in this period, from which this excerpt is taken.

It is impossible to write about any part of the McCarthy period in a clear-dated, annotated form; much crossed with much else, nothing obeyed a neat plan. . . .

But many people who were questioned acted neither good nor bad, just puzzled. How could you know that during the war a benefit for Russian War Relief wasn't as irreproachable as Bundles for Britain? You couldn't possibly have guessed, unless you were mentally disturbed, that there would come into being such a phrase as "premature anti-Fascist." The popularity of that phrase, the fact that most of America took it seriously and even pretended to understand it, must have been the forerunner of the double-talk we were to hear in the Watergate days. We, as a people, agreed in the Fifties to swallow any nonsense that was repeated often enough, without examination of its meaning or investigation into its roots.

It is no wonder then that many "respectable," meaning friendly, witnesses were often bewildered by what was wanted of them, and that many, who were convinced by the surrounding hysterical pressures that they had something to hide, moved in a dream pavanne [slow dance] trying to guess what the committees wanted them to admit. They scratched around hard for dramatic revelations. . . .

I told that to Mrs. Shipley, head of the Passport Division of the State Department, in 1953. It was that year, after my own hearing, that I had an offer to do a movie script for the producer Alexander Korda, in Lon-

don. The salary was a fifth of what I had earned before the blacklist, but we needed the money and it was no time to argue. (Korda was not the only producer who saw the chance to pick up practiced writers for little money. . . .)

It was necessary, of course, to go to Europe to consult with Korda and to write the picture. Everybody who had appeared [before HUAC] as an unfriendly witness had been denied a passport. Joe Rauh [Hellman's lawyer] suggested that I go to see Mrs. Shipley. It seemed to me a useless visit, but Rauh thought I had a chance, and when I asked why, he said he'd tell me after I had seen her.

She was a severe-looking lady with a manner made more severe by its attempt not to be. We sat awkwardly in her office while a secretary was sent off for my file. I remember murmuring something about the weather and never finishing the sentence because Mrs. Shipley was staring at me. And so we sat silent for the few minutes it took the secretary to return with a fat folder. When Mrs. Shipley opened the folder I was amazed to see three large pictures of Charles Chaplin on top. I had known Chaplin, but not well, had played tennis on his court, had once listened to an endless script he wrote and never produced, had once been on a platform with him at a meeting. . . . I admired Chaplin and liked him, but to this day I do not know why his pictures were in my file. Government agencies in those wild days probably had even more misinformation than they have now, although that can always be remedied any time invention is needed again.

Mrs. Shipley did not comment on the Chaplin pictures, but began to read a list of organizations to which I had either belonged or contributed money, and a few I had never heard of. I wanted to say that I recognized the list as coming from a book called *Red Channels,* hardly a proper source for a government agency to be using. As she read down the list, there would have been no sense denying my connection with one organization and affirming the next, and so I sat silent wondering why I had sought out this degrading hour.

Mrs. Shipley had not finished the list when she looked up and said, "Tell me, Miss Hellman, do you think most of the friendly witnesses have been telling the House Un-American Committee the truth?"

It was a most surprising question. I said no, I was sure they had not, many of them had been coached to confess what they had never done and had never seen.

Mrs. Shipley said, "Edward G. Robinson, for example?"

I said I thought so, but I wasn't sure. But there were others, Martin Berkeley for example, who said that I had been at a Communist meeting in his house. I was never at his house and didn't believe I ever met him.

I said, "The kiddies have been playing games on all of you, Mrs. Shipley, and you deserve the tricks they played because you pushed them into it."

Mrs. Shipley did not seem angry. She was thoughtful as she riffled through the rest of my file, seemingly looking for something she knew was there. Then she said, "I've suspected many of them were lying. They will be punished for it."

I said, "I don't think that's the way the world is going. It's people like me who need

jobs. That's why I came here not wanting to come."

She said, "I can see that," and was close to a smile. When the near smile had been suppressed she said, "When you go to Europe do you see political people?"

I said I didn't know many, except Louis Aragon and his wife Elsa Triolet, and a few men who had fought in Spain.

She said, "Please write me a letter saying that and that you will take no part in political movements." I thought about that for a while, not understanding it, looking for the trick. Then I said, "I've never had any part in European political movements, except to be anti-Nazi and anti-Fascist. Certainly I'll write you just that. But I can't promise not to see old friends."

She rose. "Thank you." She moved toward the door. "You will be issued a limited passport. . . . If you wish to stay in Europe longer because of your cinema work, you will have to apply here again."

She went out of the room. A secretary appeared and opened another door for me into the hall. . . . Rauh was waiting on a bench.

He got up. "You got the passport."

"Yes."

As we left the building, he grinned. "I think you're the only unfriendly witness who has gotten one."

"Why were you so sure I would get it? . . ."

"Because," he said, "one Puritan lady in power recognized another Puritan lady in trouble. Puritan ladies have to believe that other Puritan ladies don't lie." . . .

From Scoundrel Time *by Lillian Hellman. Copyright ©1976 by Lillian Hellman. By permission of Little, Brown & Company.*

Critical Thinking

1. Why, according to Hellman, did many "friendly witnesses" not tell the truth at HUAC hearings?
2. How did the HUAC hearings make it both necessary and almost impossible for Hellman to travel to England?
3. Why might knowing "a few men who fought in Spain" have been dangerous during the McCarthy era?

Connecting History and Literature

Answer one question with a brief essay.

A. What is the point of Hellman's question: "How could you know that during the war a benefit for Russian War Relief wasn't as irreproachable as Bundles for Britain?"

B. *Scoundrel Time* was attacked by many as a falsification of history. Why, do you think, did this book anger many people?

WORKSHEET 32
The Seizure of Alcatraz Island

Native Americans in northern California consider Alcatraz Island a sacred place. When the federal government abandoned its prison on Alcatraz, Native Americans living in the area decided to reassert their rights to the island. From November 1969 to June 1971, Indian people occupied Alcatraz Island. In 1969 the protesters composed a "Proclamation to the Great White Father and All His People," reprinted below.

We, the native Americans, re-claim the land known as Alcatraz Island in the name of all American Indians by right of discovery.

We wish to be fair and honorable in our dealings with the Caucasian inhabitants of this land, and hereby offer the following treaty:

We will purchase said Alcatraz Island for twenty-four dollars ($24) in glass beads and red cloth, a precedent set by the white man's purchase of [Manhattan Island] about 300 years ago. We know that $24 in trade goods for these 16 acres is more than was paid when Manhattan Island was sold, but we know that land values have risen over the years. Our offer of $1.24 per acre is greater than the 47¢ per acre that the white men are now paying the California Indians for their land.

We will give to the inhabitants of this island a portion of that land for their own, to be held in trust by the American Indian Affairs and by the Bureau of Caucasian Affairs to hold in perpetuity—for as long as the sun shall rise and the rivers go down to the sea.

We will further guide the inhabitants in the proper way of living. We will offer them our religion, our education, our life-ways, in order to help them achieve our level of civilization and thus raise them and all their white brothers up from their savage and unhappy state. We offer this treaty in good faith and wish to be fair and honorable in our dealings with all white men . . . .

We feel that this so-called Alcatraz Island is more suitable than for an Indian Reservation, as determined by the white man's own standards. By this we mean that this place resembles most Indian reservations in that:

1. It is isolated from modern facilities, and without adequate means of transportation.
2. It has no fresh running water.
3. It has inadequate sanitation facilities.
4. There are no oil or mineral rights.
5. There is no industry and so unemployment is very great.
6. There are no health care facilities.
7. The soil is rocky and non-productive; and the land does not support game.
8. There are no educational facilities.
9. The population has always exceeded the land base.
10. The population has always been held as prisoners and kept dependent. . . .

From "Proclamation to the Great White Father and All his People," Documents Relating to the Indian Occupation of Alcatraz Island, November 1969 to June 1971, Box 3, National Archives.

Comprehension

1. What does the proclamation propose to do with Alcatraz Island?
2. What offer is made regarding the people living on the island?
3. To what piece of land does the proclamation compare Alcatraz Island?

Critical Thinking

4. What is irony? How does this proclamation use irony to make its point?

Name _____ Date _____

The civil rights movement helped literature about the African American experience become part of mainstream American culture. In her novel *The Women of Brewster Place* (1982), Gloria Naylor wove together stories about the people of a dead-end urban neighborhood. In this excerpt, Kiswana Browne, who lives in Brewster Place, argues with her mother over differences within the black community.

"I don't care. I still think it's downright selfish of you to be sitting over here with no phone, and sometimes we don't hear from you in two weeks—anything could happen—especially living among these people."

Kiswana snapped her head up. "What do you mean, *these people*. They're my people and yours, too, Mama—we're all black. But maybe you've forgotten that over in Linden Hills."

"That's not what I'm talking about, and you know it. These streets—this building—it's so shabby and rundown. Honey, you don't have to live like this."

"Well, this is how poor people live."

"Melanie, you're not poor."

"No, Mama, *you're* not poor. And what you have and I have are two totally different things. I don't have a husband in real estate with a five-figure income and a home in Linden Hills—*you* do. What I have is a weekly unemployment check and an overdrawn checking account at United Federal. So this studio on Brewster is all I can afford."

"Well, you could afford a lot better," Mrs. Browne snapped, "if you hadn't dropped out of college and had to resort to these dead-end clerical jobs."

"Uh-huh, I knew you'd get around to that before long." Kiswana could feel the rings of anger begin to tighten around her lower backbone, and they sent her forward onto the couch. "You'll never understand, will you? Those bourgie [middle-class] schools were counterrevolutionary. My place was in the streets with my people, fighting for equality and a better community."

"Counterrevolutionary!" Mrs. Browne was raising her voice. "Where's your revolution now, Melanie? Where are all those black revolutionaries who were shouting and demonstrating and kicking up a lot of dust with you on that campus? Huh? They're sitting in wood-paneled offices with their degrees in mahogany frames, and they won't even drive their cars past this street because the city doesn't fix potholes in this part of town."

"Mama," she said, shaking her head slowly in disbelief, "how can you—a black woman—sit there and tell me that what we fought for during the Movement wasn't important just because some people sold out?"

"Melanie, I'm not saying it wasn't important. It was damned important to stand up and say that you were proud of what you were and to get the vote and other social opportunities for every person in this country who had it due. But you kids thought you were going to turn the world upside down, and it just wasn't so. When all the smoke had cleared, you found yourself with a fistful of new federal laws and a country still full of obstacles for black people to fight their way over—just because they're black. There was no revolution, Melanie, and there will be no revolution.

"So what am I supposed to do, huh? Just throw up my hands and not care about what happens to my people? I'm not supposed to keep fighting to make things better?"

"Of course, you can. But you're going to have to fight within the system, because it and these so-called 'bourgie' schools are going to be here for a long time. And that means that you get smart like a lot of your old friends and get an important job where you can have some influence. You don't have to sell out, as you say, and work for some corporation, but you could become an assemblywoman or a civil liberties lawyer or open a freedom school in this very neighborhood. That way you could really help the community. But what help are you going to be to these people on Brewster while you're living hand-to-mouth on file-clerk jobs waiting for a revolution? You're wasting your talents, child."

"Well, I don't think they're being wasted. At least I'm here in day-to-day contact with the problems of my people. What good would I be after four or five years of a lot of white brainwashing in some phony, prestige institution, huh? I'd be like you and Daddy and those other educated blacks sitting over there in Linden Hills with a terminal case of middle class amnesia."

"You don't have to live in a slum to be concerned about social conditions, Melanie. Your father and I have been charter members of the NAACP for the last twenty-five years."

"Oh, God!" Kiswana threw her head back in exaggerated disgust. "That's being concerned? That middle-of-the-road, Uncle Tom dumping ground for black Republicans!"

"You can sneer all you want, young lady, but that organization has been working for black people since the turn of the century, and it's still working for them. Where are all those radical groups of yours that were going to put a Cadillac in every garage and Dick Gregory in the White House? I'll tell you where."

I knew you would, Kiswana thought angrily.

"They burned themselves out because they wanted too much too fast. Their goals weren't grounded in reality. And that's always been your problem." . . .

Kiswana jumped up from the couch. "Oh, God, I can't take this anymore. Trying to be something I'm not—trying to be something I'm not, Mama! Trying to be proud of my heritage and the fact that I was of African descent. If that's being what I'm not, then I say fine. But I'd rather be dead than be like you—a white man's nigger who's ashamed of being black!"

Kiswana saw streaks of gold and ebony light follow her mother's flying body out of the chair. She was swung around by the shoulders and made to face the deadly stillness in the angry woman's eyes. She was too stunned to cry out from the pain of the long fingernails that dug into her shoulders, and she was brought so close to her mother's face that she saw her reflection, distorted and wavering, in the tears that stood in the older woman's eyes. And she listened in that stillness to a story she had heard from a child.

"My grandmother," Mrs. Browne began slowly in a whisper, "was a full-blooded Iroquois, and my grandfather a free black from a long line of journeymen [skilled craftsmen] who had lived in Connecticut since the establishment of the colonies. And my father was a Bajan [person from Barbados] who came to this country as a cabin boy on a merchant mariner."

"I know all that," Kiswana said, trying to keep her lips from trembling.

"Then, know this." And the nails dug deeper into her flesh. "I am alive because of the blood of proud people who never scraped or begged or apologized for what they were. They lived asking only one thing of this world—to be allowed to be. And I learned through the blood of these people that black isn't beautiful and it isn't ugly—black is! It's not kinky hair and it's not straight hair—it just is.

"It broke my heart when you changed your name. I gave you my grandmother's name, a woman who bore nine children and educated them all, who held off six white men with a shotgun when they tried to drag one of her sons to jail for 'not knowing his place.' Yet you needed to reach into an African dictionary to find a name to make you proud.

"When I brought my babies home from the hospital, my ebony son and my golden daughter, I swore before whatever gods would listen—those of my mother's people or those of my father's people—that I would use everything I had and could ever get to see that my children were prepared to meet this world on its own terms, so that no one could sell them short and make them ashamed of what they were or how they looked—whatever they were or however they looked. And Melanie, that's not being white or red or black—that's being a mother."

From The Women of Brewster Place *by Gloria Naylor. Copyright ©1980, 1982 by Gloria Naylor. Reprinted by permission of Viking Penguin, a division of Penguin Books USA, Inc.*

Critical Thinking

1. Why did Kiswana drop out of college?
2. What did Mrs. Browne see as the successes of the civil rights movement? How did she believe it had failed?
3. What is the NAACP? Why did Kiswana criticize her mother for belonging to it?
4. What did the name "Kiswana" mean to each of these women?

Connecting History and Literature

Answer one question with a brief essay.

A. In many political and social movements, the younger members tend to be more radical than the older members. Why is this so?
B. In discussing the civil rights movement, Kiswana and her mother also discuss wealth and poverty. How are these issues linked?

WORKSHEET 33
The Gulf War

On January 12, 1991, the Senate and the House passed a joint resolution supporting American military action in the Persian Gulf. Passage of the resolution paved the way for the beginning of the Gulf War four days later. The text of this resolution is reprinted below.

. . . WHEREAS the Government of Iraq without provocation invaded and occupied the territory of Kuwait on August 2, 1990; and

WHEREAS both the House of Representatives . . . and the Senate . . . have condemned Iraq's invasion of Kuwait and declared their support for international action to reverse Iraq's aggression; and

WHEREAS Iraq's conventional, chemical, biological, and nuclear weapons and ballistic missile programs and its demonstrated willingness to use weapons of mass destruction pose a grave threat to world peace; and

WHEREAS the international community has demanded that Iraq withdraw unconditionally and immediately from Kuwait and that Kuwait's independence and legitimate government be restored; and

WHEREAS the U.N. Security Council repeatedly affirmed the inherent right of individual or collective self-defense in response to the armed attack by Iraq against Kuwait in accordance with Article 51 of the U.N. Charter; and

WHEREAS, in the absence of full compliance by Iraq with its resolutions, the U.N. Security [Council] in Resolution 678 has authorized member states of the United Nations to use all necessary means, after January 15, 1991, to uphold and implement all relevant Security Council resolutions and to restore international peace and security in the area; and

WHEREAS Iraq has persisted in its illegal occupation of, and brutal aggression against Kuwait; Now, therefore, be it

Resolved by the Senate and House of Representatives of the United States of America in Congress assembled, . . .

Section 2.

AUTHORIZATION FOR USE OF U.S. ARMED FORCES

(a) AUTHORIZATION. — The President is authorized, subject to subsection (b), to use United States Armed Forces pursuant to United Nations Security Council Resolution 678 (1990) in order to achieve implementation of Security Council resolutions 660, 661, 662, 664, 665, 666, 667, 669, 670, 674, and 677.

(b) REQUIREMENT FOR DETERMINATION THAT USE OF MILITARY FORCE IS NECESSARY.—Before exercising the authority granted in subsection (a), the President shall make available to the speaker of the House of Representatives and the President pro tempore of the Senate his determination that—

(1) the United States has used all appropriate diplomatic and other peaceful means to obtain compliance by Iraq with the United Nations Security Council resolutions cited in subsection (a); and (2) that those efforts have not been and would not be successful in obtaining such compliance. . . .

Comprehension

1. The "whereas" section of this resolution gives seven reasons for authorizing the use of force in the Persian Gulf. List them.

2. What requirements must the President meet before he actually orders the use of force?

Critical Thinking

3. Is this document a declaration of war? Explain.

WORSHEET 33

Literature

Edward Bellamy, *Looking Backward*

Edward Bellamy wrote *Looking Backward* in 1888, at a time when the rise of industry and cities was transforming this nation in ways both good and bad. In the novel, Julian West awakens in the year 2000. His host, Doctor Leete, explains how society has been reorganized to solve the economic injustices of the late 1800s.

"It is very simple," said Doctor Leete. "When innumerable [very many] different and independent persons produced the various things needful to life and comfort, endless exchanges between individuals were requisite [required]. . . . But as soon as the nation became the sole producer of all sorts of commodities, there was no need of exchanges between individuals. . . . A system of direct distribution from the national storehouses took the place of trade, and for this, money was unnecessary."

"How is the distribution managed?" I asked.

"On the simplest possible plan," replied Doctor Leete. "A credit corresponding to his share of the annual product of the nation is given to every citizen on the public books at the beginnning of each year, and a credit card issued him with which he procures [obtains] at the public storehouses, found in every community, whatever he desires whenever he desires it. . . . Perhaps you would like to see what our credit cards are like.

"You observe," he pursued as I was curiously examining the piece of pasteboard he gave me, "that this card is issued for a certain number of *dollars*. We have kept the old word but not the substance. . . . The value of what I procure on this card is checked off by the clerk, who pricks out of these tiers of squares the price of what I order." . . .

"What if you have to spend more than your card in any one year?" I asked.

"The provision is so ample that we are more likely not to spend it all," replied Dr. Leete. . . .

"If you don't spend your allowance, I suppose it accumulates?"

"That is also permitted to a certain extent. . . . But unless notice to the contrary is given, it is presumed that the citizen who does not fully expend his credit did not have occasion to do so, and the balance is turned into the general surplus."

"Such a system does not encourage saving habits on the part of citizens," I said.

"It is not intended to," was the reply. "The nation is rich. . . . No man any more has any care for the morrow, . . . for the nation guarantees the nurture, education, and comfortable maintenance of every citizen from the cradle to the grave."

"That is a sweeping guarantee!" I said. . . . "On the whole, society may be able to support all its members, but some must earn less than enough for their support, and others more. . . . How, then, do you regulate wages?" . . .

Doctor Leete did not reply till after several moments of meditative [thoughtful] silence. . . . "I can only reply that there is no idea in the modern social economy which at all corresponds with what was meant by wages in your day."

"I suppose you mean that you have no money to pay wages in," said I. "But the credit given the worker at the government storehouse answers to his wages with us. How is the amount of the credit given . . . to the workers in different lines determined? By what title does the individual claim his particular share? . . ."

"His title," replied Doctor Leete, "is his humanity. . . ."

"Do you possibly mean that all have the same share?"

"Most assuredly. . . . We leave no possible ground for any complaint of injustice . . . by requiring precisely the same measure of service from all. . . . We require of each that he shall make the same effort; that is, we demand of him the best service it is in his power to give."

From Edward Bellamy, Looking Backward *(Ticknor & Company, 1888).*

Critical Thinking

1. In Bellamy's imaginary society, what system has replaced stores and shopping?
2. What do you admire about this imaginary society? What faults do you see in it?
3. Compare how "pay" was determined in the years 1887 and 2000. In what way are the two societies' attitudes toward wages different?

Connecting History and Literature

Answer one question with a brief essay.

A. Was Bellamy's prediction about the replacement of money at all accurate? Explain.
B. In imagining a future society, Bellamy paid special attention to issues that posed problems in his own society. If you were writing a futuristic novel like Bellamy's, what issues in today's society would you address?

Worksheet Answers

Answers to Primary Source Worksheets

CHAPTER 1

Primary Source Worksheet 1

1. The houses were three or four stories high and were made of stone and mud. There was storage space on the ground floor; ladders reached to dwellings above. The Zuñi used dirt, which was abundant in their environment, to create shelters for themselves.
2. The Zuñi ate turkey, corn, beans, and squash. They were unfamiliar with fruit or fish.
3. The Zuñi had only stone arrows, mallets, and other arms made of wood. Europeans, in contrast, had guns, swords, and other metal weapons.
4. Both the Zuñi and the Anasazi lived in apartment-like dwellings with *kivas*. Both peoples also used pottery and turquoise.
5. The account does have two characteristics of primary sources: it came from an eyewitness and dates from the time of the events discussed. On the other hand, it was not written down by an eyewitness, but instead is a second-hand account.

CHAPTER 2

Primary Source Worksheet 2

1. Non-Muslims. Muslims.
2. To limit the supply of gold on the market and thus protect the price of gold.
3. Their attempt failed, and the gold trade was stopped for three years.
4. The people of Ghana were suspicious of outsiders. For example, the groves that surrounded El Ghaba were guarded against intruders. Also, the source of gold for Ghana was a closely guarded secret.

CHAPTER 3

Primary Source Worksheet 3

1. The ship had to wait seven weeks to go around the Cape because of a great storm and strong winds.
2. The farther west Magellan's fleet sailed, the more time it gained. Eventually it gained a full day.
3. They did not want the Portuguese to know that they had been around the Cape of Good Hope because, according to the Line of Demarcation, that region was under Portuguese influence.
4. Both sailed seeking a particular destination (Columbus was looking for Asia, while Magellan was looking for the Spice Islands), yet both discovered something far more important (Columbus, the Americas, and Magellan, a route around the globe).

CHAPTER 4

Primary Source Worksheet 4

1. They were starved, overworked, and treated with cruelty.
2. The Spaniards saw the Indians as expendable sources of labor, not as humans. They made no effort to treat them humanely, nor were they concerned with the high death rate.

3. He thought the Spaniards were using Christianity as an excuse to obtain additional laborers. He did think the king was sincere, since the Spaniards had to "deceive" him with this "crafty argument."
4. The Indians, as well as Spaniards of conscience, would have seen Las Casas as a saint for pointing out the crimes committed against the Indians. Landowners and other advocates of the Spanish conquest, however, would have seen him as their enemy.

CHAPTER 5

Primary Source Worksheet 5

1. The French made a large cross, hung a shield on it, and kneeled and thanked God before the cross.
2. At first the Indians were impressed with the cross and the ceremony surrounding it. However, the chief explained that the surrounding land around them was his, and the French needed to ask permission before putting up crosses.
3. They might not have had such advanced tools.
4. Possibly they wanted to show the people in France what the natives of the Americas looked like; the French may also have wanted the Indians as hostages.

CHAPTER 6

Primary Source Worksheet 6

1. As soon as the Indians knew that Smith had gone, they attacked the settlement.
2. Indians and Jamestown's leaders ate the farm animals that were left.
3. It dropped from 500 to 60.
4. Survivors ate roots, herbs, nuts, berries, some fish, and even horse skins.
5. Smith blames the starving time on the settlers' lack of hard work, thrift, and organization, not on the land itself. This is a logical explanation, for the Indians managed to live well enough on what the land provided.
6. Smith must have gotten his information from settlers who stayed behind. Because it is second-hand information, and written fifteen years after the event, his record may not be entirely accurate.

CHAPTER 7

Primary Source Worksheet 7

1. God.
2. No; God's wrath includes those who are outwardly religious.
3. God hates them, is offended by them, and thinks that they are unworthy.
4. To be "born again" in a new commitment to God.
5. Some people might have been frightened; some might have felt guilty at their misdeeds; some might have felt a powerful urge to renew their religious commitment.

CHAPTER 8

Primary Source Worksheet 8

1. Braddock was arrogantly confident of British success.

2. Franklin feared that Braddock's troops, marching in a long line through the woods, would be an easy target for an Indian ambush.

3. The enemy waited until the British soldiers were gathered together in a clearing, then surprised them by shooting from behind bushes and trees.

4. The British lost the battle and two-thirds of their soldiers. The rest fled in panic.

5. Writing many years after the battle, Franklin may have exaggerated Braddock's vanity and poor leadership. By the time he began to write his autobiography, the American colonies had already begun to clash with Britain.

CHAPTER 9

Primary Source Worksheet 9

1. The right to be taxed only with their personal consent or that of an elected representative.

2. The colonists were not represented in the House of Commons.

3. Resolution XI says that because of the restrictions on trade imposed by these acts of Parliament, colonists will not be able to buy goods from Britain.

4. The first section, in which colonists recognize their allegiance to the king and to Parliament.

CHAPTER 10

Primary Source Worksheet 10

1. Congress would appoint a governor, secretary, and court, and a general assembly would be formed.

2. 5,000 free male inhabitants of a certain age.

3. Article III declared that land and property could not be taken from Indians without their consent.

4. Article II.

5. Fugitive slaves would be reclaimed and returned to their lawful owners.

CHAPTER 11

Primary Source Worksheet 11

1. He believed that the Constitution did not adequately protect individual rights.

2. Other people wanted one, and it would protect people from an oppressive government.

3. Madison said that the power in government lay with the majority of the community.

4. While a strong government could be tyrannical and violate personal liberties, a weak government would not be able to protect people from the tyranny of the majority.

CHAPTER 12

Primary Source Worksheet 12

1. The minority possess equal rights, which must be protected by the law.

2. Equal justice for all, the right to free elections, freedom of religion, and trial by jury.

3. He called for peace, commerce, and honest friendship with all nations and entangling alliances with none.

4. A government that allows freedom of speech can depend on reason rather than oppression to combat those who criticize the government.

5. Possible answer: "While we are in the midst of this dispute with France, we must do whatever is necessary to keep the country united; we cannot let people criticize the government or its leaders."

CHAPTER 13

Primary Source Worksheet 13

1. "Great Father" was the British king and "Father" was his representative.

2. Retreat from British land even though the enemy was not in sight.

3. He compared the British to a frightened animal that puts its tail between its legs and runs off.

4. He wanted the British to remain; the Shawnee would retreat with them if defeated by the Americans. If the British didn't remain, he wanted them to leave behind the arms and ammunition sent to the Shawnee by the king.

5. No. In 1794, when the Shawnee retreated to the British fort, the British shut the gates against them.

6. To defend Shawnee lands, with or without British help.

CHAPTER 14

Primary Source Worksheet 14

1. Work begins at five in the morning and ends at seven at night.

2. The workers have a half-hour for breakfast and a half-hour or forty-five minutes for dinner, depending on the season of the year. Many go directly to bed because they are so tired.

3. The factory is extremely noisy and thus could damage the workers' hearing. The air inside the factory is full of fibers and dust, which are harmful to the workers' lungs.

4. The writer strongly disapproves of the mill system. He points out that rushing the workers through their meals is not good for their health. He also repeats several times that a thirteen-hour work day is too long. Words like "frightful" and "infernal" describe the noise level of the factory.

5. Students might suggest stuffing their ears with cotton, saving money so that they could leave as soon as possible, forming a union, or relying on prayer.

CHAPTER 15

Primary Source Worksheet 15

1. Webster claimed that if the states were supreme, the national government would have to answer to 24 masters at the same time, which would be impossible. He also said that the Constitution came from the people and the government belonged to the people.

2. Webster believed that if Liberty came first, there probably would be no Union.

3. ". . . states dissevered, discordant, belligerent; on a land rent with civil feuds, or drenched, it may be, in fraternal blood!"

4. Possible answers include abortion, nuclear power and weapons, and environmental concerns. Most issues are not based so much on sectional differences as on ideological differences.

CHAPTER 16

Primary Source Worksheet 16

1. Insane persons were being kept in cages, stalls, and unheated rooms, sometimes in chains and sometimes without clothing.

2. The legislature had the power to make laws to improve the conditions of the insane.

3. She probably would have objected, arguing that it was inappropriate to house ill persons with prisoners because the former had done nothing wrong and should not be punished.

4. In many cases, they are unable to speak for themselves or improve their own lives.

CHAPTER 17

Primary Source Worksheet 17

1. He saw boundless prairies, large rivers, herds of buffalo, deer, and wild horses, and mighty plains.

2. Upton mentioned hard marches, disease, and the anticipation of hard fighting and possible death.

3. It was eager to fight.

4. He believed that the Mexicans would, and should, defend their country from invasion, yet he also held Mexicans responsible for the war.

5. Yes; he said he was happy with his situation and he seemed to like the country and the traveling.

6. He felt compassion for the soldiers who would die in battle or from disease. He seemed to have made peace with the possibility of his own death, and hoped that he would perform his duty to the end.

7. Responses should reflect Upton's willingness to be an American soldier and his belief that he was right to fight in the war. They might also reflect his enjoyment of new places, his appreciation of nature, and his compassion for others.

CHAPTER 18

Primary Source Worksheet 18

1. The phrase "each State acting in its sovereign and independent character."

2. Article I, Section 8, Clause 1.

3. Tariffs could not be used to promote or foster industry, and they were to be uniform throughout the Confederate States.

4. Article IV, Section 3, Clause 3.

5. The South, primarily agrarian, wanted lower tariffs because the region had little manufacturing to protect from foreign competition and because tariffs raised prices on imported goods. The South believed that government should not meddle in business.

CHAPTER 19

Primary Source Worksheet 19

1. He was a great mimic with an excellent sense of humor, and he liked to amuse people.

2. Lincoln was frustrated with General Meade; he could see the mistakes Meade was making, whereas Meade could not.

3. Chandler seemed to respect, even love, Lincoln. He clearly enjoyed Lincoln's humor and sympathized with his frustration over Union generals.

4. Yes; Lincoln was searching for a Union general who would pursue and destroy Lee's army.

CHAPTER 20

Primary Source Worksheet 20

1. He said the blacks should continue to work for him and he would protect them from "bad white men"; he tried to convince them to sign a work contract they could not read; he paid them little or nothing for their work.

2. He was afraid his former master would trick him into signing a contract that would be to his disadvantage.

3. He refused to sign the work contract; he asked his master for part of what they harvested; he refused to carry a pass when he left the plantation; he declared that he did not belong to anyone, even though he was beaten up by whites for saying so.

4. Blacks could not be called free as we know it. Whites tried to take advantage of their ignorance, intimidate them, or even kill them.

5. The federal government was concerned about the condition of the former slaves. As a former slave, Adams had first-hand knowledge of their living conditions.

CHAPTER 21

Primary Source Worksheet 21

1. Leave it to their families; bequeath it for public purposes after death; administer it during their lifetime for the public good.

2. The third way, because he sees it as a cure for the unequal distribution of wealth.

3. He said that when great sums are bequeathed, they often bring more harm than good to the recipients.

4. Yes; he gave away $350 million to help establish libraries, schools, and a world peace organization.

5. It provides social justification for the making of great fortunes.

6. Possible arguments: Many wealthy people do not give away their fortunes for the public good; what one person considers "the public good" may not be generally agreed upon; people who need help the most may not benefit from this use of wealth.

CHAPTER 22

Primary Source Worksheet 22

1. Tammany bosses corrupted the people; votes were bought by kindness or when necessary by intimidation.

2. They were natural leaders and good-natured kindly men who offered real charity and helped people in trouble, at first.

3. As they grew rich and powerful, they collected money for their "goodness"; they sacrificed education and public health; they planted vice in the neighborhoods; and they eventually sold out their own people.

4. Many of the people in cities were immigrants. Because they received some real help from the bosses and because they lacked knowledge of the language and laws, immigrants were not likely to openly criticize Tammany bosses.

5. Students may say that Steffens' words indicate he thought honest government was more important. Political machines did more harm than good, i.e., they weren't interested in the larger public; candidates won votes not on their qualifications, but through "petty privileges" or intimidation; and the corruption of bosses infected other people and undermined the welfare of the communities.

CHAPTER 23

Primary Source Worksheet 23

1. They look to men for protection.
2. They face being trampled, being struck by lightning in a thunderstorm, or falling from their horses.
3. They catch up to the leaders of the herd and then head them off. The rest of the herd stops when the leaders of the herd stop.
4. He has great respect for the cowboys. Stopping a stampede is hard and dangerous work.
5. Students may suggest an ability to remain calm in the face of wild excitement (such as a stampede), physical courage, and persistence.

CHAPTER 24

Primary Source Worksheet 24

1. Farming had become unprofitable. Although farmers were working hard, they were sinking more and more into debt, until the mortgages finally took their farms. Hired workers made more money than the farm owner.
2. Throughout the country, i.e., in the East, the South, the Midwest, and the West.
3. Farmers were planning to take immediate action, by whatever social combinations or united political action necessary, to alleviate their suffering.
4. Bad weather; drop in crop prices (due to increase in farm output at home and abroad); high cost of farm machinery; high cost of transporting crops by railroad.
5. Farmers formed the Grange and the Farmers' Alliance and helped to create the People's Party (Populist Party). They also pushed to increase the supply of silver.

CHAPTER 25

Primary Source Worksheet 25

1. German policy of unrestricted submarine warfare.
2. Vindication of human rights.
3. Many people of German descent lived in the United States; war was against the German government, not the German people.
4. To fight for democracy, to bring peace and safety to all nations, to make the world free.
5. Americans can dedicate themselves to fight for the principles upon which the nation was founded and to secure world peace.

CHAPTER 26

Primary Source Worksheet 26

1. Vanzetti believed that Judge Thayer was "prejudiced" and "cruel," that he had prejudged them as radicals before the trial began, and that he had publicly expressed hostility and "despisement" against them.

2. He claimed he was not guilty of bloodshed but was "guilty" of being a radical and an Italian.
3. Answers will vary. Students may mention the atmosphere of hysteria, prejudiced judges and jurors, unjustified executions of innocent parties. Others may support the outcome of the trial, arguing that radicals are dangerous to society.

CHAPTER 27

Primary Source Worksheet 27

1. Many families evicted from their apartments had to live crowded in with relatives; lived in unheated homes because they couldn't afford coal; ate meat only once a week, if at all.
2. They felt inadequate, as though they would not be able to remember basic rules of employment.
3. The worst thing was the fact that it went on for so long. Men could handle being unemployed for a few months, but being out of work for years meant that many ended up living on park benches and eating in soup kitchens.
4. State and local governments and charitable groups such as the Red Cross did the most, but there was never enough help for all those who needed it.

CHAPTER 28

Primary Source Worksheet 28

1. Students may mention any of the following: cultural devastation, slavery, physical suffering, abrupt emancipation, migration, joblessness, insecurity, longing, disillusionment, bewilderment.
2. *Positive experiences:* working together in labor unions and demanding relief measures and adequate housing. *Negative experiences:* realizing that most blacks are in positions of economic inferiority to whites on every level.
3. White Americans must realize their common bond with blacks, that they struggle together for a good life. If blacks are not allowed to succeed, America will be the loser.

CHAPTER 29

Primary Source Worksheet 29

1. The awful waste and destruction, even aside from the loss of human life; everything is expendable.
2. Because men and equipment were flowing from England in such a gigantic stream.
3. Some students may focus on the mixture of sleeping and dead men on the beach. Some may think the description of the armada is most powerful.

CHAPTER 30

Primary Source Worksheet 30

1. He told the colonel he had moved his position, knowing the colonel couldn't see that he hadn't. He did it to avoid enemy fire and thus save his life and the lives of his men.

2. He realized that he had enjoyed doing some things in Vietnam which he was ashamed of when he was in an "English" country.

3. He had Vietnam civilians walk point, rather than any of his men, so they would be the first to encounter any ambushes or booby traps.

4. Some Americans serving in Vietnam felt that they were suffering and dying to protect the freedoms Americans enjoyed at home, and they resented the lack of support they received.

CHAPTER 31

Primary Source Worksheet 31

1. The FBI was tracing money paid to the burglars by Nixon's re-election committee, and the number of people who had to take part in the cover-up was growing.

2. To have the CIA tell the FBI to drop the investigation.

3. The tapes implicated Pat Gray, head of the FBI, and Walters, Deputy Director of the CIA, in addition to the President and Haldeman.

4. Nixon knowingly obstructed justice in his cover-up; he used government agencies to violate constitutional rights of citizens; he illegally withheld evidence from Congress.

5. It proved that dishonest officials, no matter how high their office, could not undermine the government established by the Constitution.

CHAPTER 32

Primary Source Worksheet 32

1. Native Americans should buy it for $24.

2. It offers to teach them Indian ways in order to raise their level of civilization.

3. An Indian reservation.

4. Irony is saying something other than what is meant. Through their "offer" to buy Alcatraz Island and "civilize" its inhabitants, the writers of the proclamation are reminding people of past abuses against Native Americans.

CHAPTER 33

Primary Source Worksheet 33

1. Iraq's occupation of Kuwait, Congress's earlier condemnation of that invasion, Iraq's threat to world peace, other nations' demands for an Iraqi withdrawal, the UN's support for the right of self-defense, UN Resolution 678 authorizing UN members to enforce UN resolutions, and Iraq's refusal to withdraw from Kuwait.

2. The President must inform the House and Senate leaders that the United States has tried all peaceful means to convince Iraq to withdraw, and that these efforts have failed.

3. In effect it was very similar to a declaration of war, since it paved the way for the start of hostilities. Yet it was not a declaration of war because the original authorization to use force against Iraq came from the United Nations.

Answers to Literature Worksheets

CHAPTER 1

Literature Worksheet 1

1. The song expresses a belief in life after death when it says "truly we die not/because we will live, we will rise."

2. Burning the dead is explained in the repeated phrases, "flame-coloured" or "fire-coloured" birds and butterflies, which evoke the image of fire.

A. These songs and stories tell us about the lives and beliefs of those peoples.

B. Students should indicate that translations are not as reliable as the original language. There may be no exact or comparable words in the new language. Translators use their own judgment and may make mistakes. Often more than one "correct" version can be handed down.

CHAPTER 2

Literature Worksheet 2

1. All of them wanted to receive his cow-tail switch.

2. The older sons had forgotten about Ogaloussa. The youngest son's first words had been to ask for his father.

3. The living can and should keep alive those who have died by keeping them in their memories.

A. Students may argue that the simplicity and directness of the story make the story effective.

B. One advantage of oral tradition is that a story-teller can use facial gestures and inflection to add meaning to a story. A potential disadvantage is that stories will be altered as they are passed from person to person.

CHAPTER 3

Literature Worksheet 3

1. They want Escobar to convince the local Indians to return to their village and to continue mining gold.

2. They regard the Indians as sources of labor.

3. He does not approve of the Spaniards' mistreatment of the Indians and does not want to betray them.

A. The excerpt shows that Spain valued American gold.

B. The job of the missionaries was not to conquer the Indians or exploit their labor but to convert them.

CHAPTER 4

Literature Worksheet 4

1. They were disguised as peddlers.

2. He knew the Indians' language. He went ahead of the group to find out news and get directions from the Indians.

3. They thought the travelers were shamans. This meant that the Indians would respect and fear the travelers, not harm them.

A. They had been part of the Narváez expedition to find the Rio Grande. The expedition had been shipwrecked.

B. No. The Spanish did not find the precious metals they sought.

CHAPTER 5

Literature Worksheet 5

1. Spendlove said that a wall was needed to protect the colonists' possessions. Berry said that the colonists had to make a show of force in order to hold on to their land.

2. The two goals were to convert the Indians or to establish control over the land. Converting the Indians would be easier without a wall; maintaining control over the land would be easier with the wall.

3. He feared that the wall would keep the colonists in as well as the Indians out.

4. He wanted the colonists to build friendly relations with the Indians rather than fight them.

A. According to Richard Hakluyt, colonies would provide a place to send petty criminals, sites for overseas bases, markets for English exports, and new converts to Protestant Christianity.

B. The colonists fear the Indians and do not trust them, yet they also realize the desirability of cooperating with the Indians if possible.

CHAPTER 6

Literature Worksheet 6

1. The new arrivals were singing, and had a drum and a scarlet cloak. The settlers were silent and starving.

2. Some settlers were so weak from hunger and disease that they would soon die.

3. Because they had not eaten in so long, the sight of food made them ill.

A. The previous winter had been a time of starvation and pestilence. The settlers had been afraid to leave the fort.

B. To survive, the colonies needed to be resupplied from England by ship. Also, if England expected to import any products from its colonies, these too had to travel by ship.

CHAPTER 7

Literature Worksheet 7

1. Time is most precious. Lost time is never found again, and what seems like enough time is never as much as we think. If we get up late, we must rush all day to complete what has to be done.

2. Through diligence, or hard work, we will never starve or be in debt and will have good luck. God rewards those who work hard.

3. Leisure means using time to do something useful; it is not laziness or wasting time. Only people who work hard will gain leisure.

A. Students who agree with Franklin may argue that hard work is still important to success. Students who disagree may argue that even hard work doesn't always bring success, and enjoyment of friends and family is more important than working long hours.

B. The colonies provided many economic opportunities for those persons able and willing to work hard.

CHAPTER 8

Literature Worksheet 8

1. Hot weather, mosquitoes, fear of discovery by the French, fatigue.

2. Because his "sweaty and raffish" troops had a bedraggled look.

3. He viewed him as a hero and as a man possessed of great energy and fierce determination.

A. Indians fought on both sides during the British-French conflicts.

B. The war resulted from British-French rivalry over their American territories and especially the Ohio Valley. The war ended with a British victory and the end of France's North American empire.

CHAPTER 9

Literature Worksheet 9

1. To warn the colonists of the approach of the British.

2. She faced danger from thieves and from the British; also, riding long distances on horseback at night is dangerous.

3. She was excited and proud of what she had accomplished.

A. The militias were formed starting in 1774. Many who joined the militias believed that a show of force by the colonists would force the British to repeal the Intolerable Acts. Others saw the militias as the means by which Americans would gain independence.

B. Because the fighting took place near Americans' homes, the Americans had strong motivation to fight and knew how to organize and communicate among themselves.

CHAPTER 10

Literature Worksheet 10

1. He believed it was prudent to get rid of it before any Patriot neighbors saw it. He no longer felt as loyal to the king as his father did.

2. His father asserted his right to support the king.

3. Patriots are presented as threatening and bullying toward Loyalists.

4. The conflict caused a split within the family.

A. The American people were divided, some favoring independence, some remaining loyal to Britain, and some neutral.

B. The Patriots could not rely on all colonists for support; they also had to worry about Loyalist spies.

CHAPTER 11

Literature Worksheet 11

1. Virginia would be the ninth state to ratify the Constitution, making it the law of the land.

2. He had refused to sign the Constitution at the Convention in Philadelphia and was assumed to be an Antifederalist.

3. Antifederalists wanted to add amendments—a bill of rights—before agreeing to ratify the Constitution. Federalists who wanted a bill of rights thought it could be added afterwards.

A. Having fought for independence from a central government that had violated their rights, Americans were naturally suspicious of government. Yet the experience of the Confederation government showed the need for a strong central government.

B. Americans disagreed over such issues as how to represent people and states in the legislature and how much power the national government should have. The only way to obtain the necessary support was to compromise on these and other issues.

CHAPTER 12

Literature Worksheet 12

1. The people were different and were dressed differently; the town was larger and busier; his house was now uninhabited. The nearby mountains, the Hudson River, and other natural features had not changed.

2. They were surprised and confused by his appearance. Some thought he was mentally ill.

3. The Revolutionary War, America's Declaration of Independence, and the establishment of a new United States government.

A. Washington's election as President; the creation of the Cabinet; the new nation's economic problems; Hamilton's economic plan.

B. Students may suggest events relating to politics, science, economics, technology, society, or other areas.

CHAPTER 13

Literature Worksheet 13

1. Their husbands traded for the goods they needed. Money was used to pay taxes.

2. There were wolves, snakes, big cats, and bears; hostile Indians also posed a threat.

3. They could join trading trains, trapping parties, Army exploring expeditions, or a crew of rivermen.

A. Bravery, self-sufficiency, capacity for hard work, willingness to endure loneliness.

B. The country as a whole worked for a living, and people were proud of the work they did.

CHAPTER 14

Literature Worksheet 14

1. She said they were too well treated to want to rebel. Students may suggest that she was deluding herself, since people are unlikely to support their own enslavement under any conditions.

2. They decide to hang any plotters, crack down on slaves' movement, and force anti-slavery whites and free blacks out of the state.

3. Vyry could not believe at first and then became greatly upset. Aunt Sally tried to reassure Vyry and then prayed for deliverance. Students may suggest that slaveowners probably were unable to see that slaves were human beings with the same emotional ties as whites.

A. The invention of the cotton gin made cotton-growing more profitable. The demand for slaves to pick cotton rose.

B. Turner led a slave rebellion in Virginia in 1831 that resulted in dozen's of deaths. After the rebellion, states passed harsh laws denying slaves the few freedoms they once had.

CHAPTER 15

Literature Worksheet 15

1. She saw that everyone appeared fearful and sad, and that many people were crying.

2. Fatigue, hunger, disease, homesickness, and cold.

3. Students may suggest that she wanted the soldiers to understand that the Creek were a proud, strong people.

4. She remembered the kinds and amounts of food they had at home. She remembered these things because she was very hungry during the journey.

A. Lands east of the Mississippi were seen as more valuable than lands west of the Mississippi. In 1830 Congress passed the Indian Removal Act, which called for the Indians to be relocated to the less-valuable lands.

B. Some moved peacefully. Others, such as the Sauk and Seminole, resisted relocation, but their resistance was not successful.

CHAPTER 16

Literature Worksheet 16

1. The judge, instead of hearing evidence on both sides of the case and allowing the jury to decide the case, ordered the jury to find her guilty.

2. The jury was not made up of her peers; it was entirely male.

3. A harsh penalty would call attention to her case and help her publicize her campaign for women's suffrage.

A. Both groups were demanding greater rights for persons denied equal treatment. Also, many people in the women's rights movement were also members of the abolitionist movement.

B. Students may suggest that a change in popular attitudes had to precede the change in the Constitution, and that changing attitudes can take a very long time.

CHAPTER 17

Literature Worksheet 17

1. He called them lazy, careless with money, unproductive, suspicious of foreigners, prejudiced against non-Catholics, and cruel to Indians.

2. No Protestant had any political rights; the native Californians were suspicious of outsiders; leading citizens were civil officers, while Indians did all the hard work for food and some cloth.

3. Dana's attitudes do suggest that he believed western territories would be better off as part of the United States.

A. Unlike Spain, Mexico encouraged trade with the United States.

B. American settlers in Texas won independence from Mexico; American traders were conducting business in California; American settlers were moving west over the Oregon Trail.

CHAPTER 18

Literature Worksheet 18

1. It was the start of a reign of terror by slavecatchers against northern blacks.

2. The treatment of former slaves differed greatly, according to circumstances.

3. Presumably the Flints saw Jacobs as their property, not as a person.

A. To protect her family and friends in the South, and those who had helped her escape.

B. Former slaves were still in danger of being caught and returned.

CHAPTER 19

Literature Worksheet 19

1. They needed shoes.

2. Stuart and his cavalry were late. Lee needed Stuart to find out about Union movements.

3. Lee gave the order when he saw a chance to drive the Union line back.

A. Lee hoped that an invasion of the North would discourage northerners and bring European backing for the South. He also needed supplies for his men.

B. Lee's troops were defeated but managed to escape.

CHAPTER 20

Literature Worksheet 20

1. Mrs. Blake's brocade dress, lace cap, rings; the family portraits; references to 300 servants; a house where Washington had slept; the fact that she had been a "southern belle."

2. The time before the Confederate states seceded.

3. She believed that the Confederacy still existed, with new presidents chosen regularly.

A. Slavery no longer existed; many of the region's cities and plantations had been destroyed during the Civil War; the region was occupied by U.S. troops.

B. Students may conclude that Carraway's own background had taught him to respect this way of life and to understand why the family had preserved the mother's illusions.

CHAPTER 21

Literature Worksheet 21

1. His comments about the attitudes of people in Wall Street toward the strikers (joking, swearing, etc.); his portrayal of Dryfoos acquiring a fortune while the workers are taking a chance by striking.

2. That strikes are always "bad business," that the new elevated trains make the streetcars less necessary and thereby weaken the strikers' chances.

3. The realistic settings on the street and in the office; the dialogue between Conrad and Dryfoos, reflecting the way people really speak.

A. Owners wanted to keep profits high by working people hard and paying them little. Workers organized unions and went out on strike to improve pay and working conditions.

B. The government did not see itself as responsible for protecting workers; thus it tended to side with owners against striking workers.

CHAPTER 22

Literature Worksheet 22

1. The streets to the river ended in dead ends with fences.

2. They probably were homesick; also, some probably were unhappy about their lives in America.

3. That person might have been referring to the sense of freedom in this nation, or the economic opportunity.

A. There are references to the Slavs, to eastern European rivers such as the Vistula, Bug, and Volga, and to the Polish and Russian languages.

B. They did not have enough money to move to more wealthy areas; there were more economic opportunities for them in the city; living near other emigrants from their home country eased the transition to life in America.

CHAPTER 23

Literature Worksheet 23

1. The Kiowas used buffalo hides for tipis, clothes, and moccasins. They ate buffalo meat. They used buffalo hide or bladders or stomachs to store things. They also used buffalo in religious ceremonies.

2. The buffalo tore up the railroad tracks and gardens and chased the cattle off the ranges.

3. The ending might symbolize the desire to return to a better life, one without white settlers. It might also symbolize the hope that one day the buffalo would return to the plains.

A. Unlike the white settlers, the Kiowas only killed as many buffalo as they needed to fulfill their requirements for food, shelter, and other purposes. The Kiowas and buffalo coexisted on the plains.

B. By killing the buffalo, whites deprived the Indians of their main source of food and shelter.

CHAPTER 24

Literature Worksheet 24

1. He had expected legislators to be dedicated, hardworking, and honest; to discuss issues seriously and make big decisions. Instead he found that many laws were made in backroom deals and that legislators were absent much of the time.

2. Some of the people who were classified as "politicians" were friendly, pleasant, and easy-going.

3. Disgusted at the political situation, Steffens became a reform journalist.

A. They can uncover corruption and other abuses of power and inform the public of these problems so that the public will support reform efforts.

B. They promoted political reforms, such as the initiative, referendum, recall, and women's suffrage; economic reforms, such as antitrust laws; and social reforms, such as protection for workers and women with dependent children.

CHAPTER 25

Literature Worksheet 25

1. They probably were bored and unhappy where they were. They may have been excited at the thought of joining battle.

2. From the movies.

3. He found the atmosphere exciting and imagined that he would become a hero. Probably many soldiers, at least at the start of the war, regarded going to war as an adventure.

A. The United States joined the war on April 6, 1917, after a series of German provocations, including the sinking of the *Lusitania*.

B. The paragraph describes physical discomfort and the sense of being a small part of a large group; these elements create an ominous mood designed to prepare readers for the fighting ahead.

CHAPTER 26

Literature Worksheet 26

1. Gatsby claims that he lost money in a financial panic during the war and then made more money quickly.
2. Daisy does seem to have been impressed. Nick noted the opulence of Gatsby's surroundings but was more interested in observing Gatsby himself.
3. He was self-conscious and showed off his possessions to impress Daisy.
A. He lives in an opulent mansion with a garden and swimming pool; he also entertains lavishly.
B. Gatsby loves Daisy more than his possessions. Fitzgerald is arguing that material wealth will not buy happiness.

CHAPTER 27

Literature Worksheet 27

1. "Black Friday" in the 1890s and the Panic of 1907.
2. Scenes of New York at the time of the crash, reactions to the first drop of the stock market in September, and the effects of the crash on people.
3. Greed and an unhealthy economy.
A. The crash triggered the Depression. The crash was one of many symptoms of economic trouble and thus was only one of the causes of the Depression.
B. When people lose faith in the economy, as happened in 1929, their actions can bring about the economic collapse they fear. In contrast, public confidence in the economy can make the economy healthier.

CHAPTER 28

Literature Worksheet 28

1. To symbolize her love for the young man, who had gone away.
2. He wanted her to move away; she wanted him to move in with her and her father.
3. They learned of the power and durability of love.
A. People coming to America felt torn between the customs of their home country and the customs of America.
B. The story contains elements of Chinese culture, yet it is set in the United States and deals with the experiences of Chinese Americans. Thus it can be seen as a Chinese, American, *and* Chinese American story.

CHAPTER 29

Literature Worksheet 29

1. Some were defiant and wanted to fight; some hid; and others gave up and followed orders.
2. The restrictions disrupted the normal flow of daily life, moved Jews from their houses, invalidated their working cards, and confined them to a manageable area.
3. He believed the Jews were being taken to their deaths.
A. Germany had seized western Poland in 1939. It had taken control of the rest of Poland in its invasion of the Soviet Union in 1941.
B. The deportation and murder of Warsaw Jews was one part of Germany's plan of genocide against European Jews.

CHAPTER 30

Literature Worksheet 30

1. He knew many other Latins, including Cubans and Mexicans, as well as Spaniards and African Americans.
2. He was not able to travel to visit the rest of his family. Some performers he admired were hurt by the revolution.
3. Raúl supported the revolution, thinking that socialism was the cure for society's problems. Cesar believed that more people were hurt than helped by the new regime.
4. They equated Castro and his movement with the Loyalist cause in Spain, recalling the political persecution under Franco's Fascist regime in Spain.
A. After leading the 1959 revolution in Cuba, Castro became allied with the Soviet Union. The United States tried to overthrow Castro, and, later, the Soviet Union tried to establish missile bases in Cuba.
B. Many of these people left Cuba because of the revolution and its effects on Cuban society; they blamed Castro for forcing them to leave their homes.

CHAPTER 31

Literature Worksheet 31

1. Because they were puzzled by the questions and accusations; because the questioners applied pressure to make them reveal something; because the questions made them feel guilty even when they were not.
2. Because she was blacklisted, she could not get screenwriting jobs in Hollywood; because she had been an "unfriendly" witness, she was not likely to get a passport.
3. Because Americans who fought in the Spanish Civil War fought with the Loyalists, an anti-Fascist group that included some Communists. Also, the Loyalists were given help by the Soviet Union.
A. Both the Soviet Union and Britain were American allies in World War II. Yet after the war, people who had helped the Soviets were suspected of Communist sympathies.
B. People's feelings on the issues it discusses were especially strong. People on both sides of the debate feared that American democracy was in danger, either from Communist subversion or from anti-Communist oppression.

CHAPTER 32

Literature Worksheet 32

1. To join the "revolutionary" side of the civil rights movement; she thought her school was "counterrevolutionary."
2. People standing up for their rights, new federal laws, more opportunities in society. The movement's more radical promises were not fulfilled because they were not based in reality.
3. The National Association for the Advancement of Colored People. Kiswana saw it as too conservative.
4. To Melanie, it meant a celebration of her African heritage; to her mother, it meant a rejection of their family's history.
A. Some people would argue that older persons, having had more experience in the world, better understand the difference between what sort of change is desirable and what is possible. Other people would argue that younger persons, not having accommodated themselves to the existing state of affairs, are more committed to making real, rather than cosmetic, changes.

B. One effect of the denial of civil rights to African Americans was to deny them equal economic opportunity. African Americans remained, on the whole, poorer than white Americans.

CHAPTER 33

Literature Worksheet 33

1. Each person has a credit card, which entitles him or her to an almost unlimited amount of products at national storehouses; the card keeps track of the products.

2. Students might admire the ideal of common humanity, providing for all members of society, and requiring from each person his or her best effort. They might find fault with the lack of competition.

3. In the year 2000, there is no "pay" because there is no differential system of wages. Each person is entitled to the same share.

A. Credit and bank cards are being widely used today in place of cash. However, money still exists.

B. Possible answers include overpopulation, environmental damage, the threat of nuclear war, and violence.